THE CLEAR & SIMPLE
WINE GUIDE

THE
CLEAR &
SIMPLE
WINE GUIDE

Louis J. DiGiacomo

STACKPOLE BOOKS

Copyright © 1981 by Louis J. DiGiacomo

Published by
STACKPOLE BOOKS
Cameron and Kelker Streets
P.O. Box 1831
Harrisburg, Pa. 17105

Published simultaneously in Don Mills, Ontario, Canada
by Thomas Nelson & Sons, Ltd.

Printed in the U.S.A.

Library of Congress Cataloging in Publication Data

DiGiacomo, Louis J., 1926–
  The clear and simple wine guide.

  Bibliography: p.
  1. Wine and wine making. I. Title.
TP548.D44 1981   641.2'22   81-5819
ISBN 0-8117-2082-9   AACR2

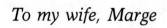

To my wife, Marge

Contents

Acknowledgments

I wish to thank and acknowledge the contributions of my very good friends, F. Curtis Davis, Jr., Esq. of Philadelphia, Pa. for the photographic work, Bob & Jean Brown of Ferndale, Pa. for the line drawings and my secretary, Elaine Sobieski of Philadelphia, Pa. for the typing of many of the original drafts of this work.

Nothing more excellent or valuable than wine was ever granted by the gods to man.

Plato

1

Introduction

Is This Book for You?

If you are a wine expert, read no further. If you know little or nothing about wine, this book is for you. It is a concise digest of basic wine facts and information. In the few hours it will take you to read this volume, you will learn more about wine than 99.44% of the people in America. It will not make you an expert or connoisseur, but your friends will think you are. It is primarily a book for self instruction, a "how to do it" book. In addition to the basic wine information it provides, it will guide and direct you with a minimum of trial and error wheel spinning, to learn more if you are so inclined.

Have you ever drunk a glass of wine in a restaurant or at a friend's house and commented, "That was very good. I'll have to buy a bottle"? Then you either promptly forgot about it or you forgot the name of the wine you enjoyed. Have you been too embarrassed to walk into a wine store to inquire about a good table wine for fear of demonstrating your total ignorance of the subject?

Have you been intimidated or cowed by a restaurant wine list or wine steward? Are you so self-conscious about your lack of knowledge about wine that you hesitate even to ask to see the wine list? If you do muster up enough courage to ask for it, do you order the wine by number because you can't pronounce most of the wines? Are you in serious trouble if the wines are not numbered; then you have to order a Burgundy which is the only one you can pronounce with confidence? Are the names Pouilly Fuisse, Cabernet Sauvignon, Pinot Noir, Beaujolais, or even Chablis as unfathomable as the medical terms used by doctors?

If your answer is "yes" to any of these questions, then this book is for you.

Where Do You Start?

The obvious question in learning about wine is "where and how do I start?" The almost as obvious answer is "buy a book." Since you have bought this book, you have already started and are well on your way. Although the technical study of wine, its chemical properties, and production is complex, wine appreciation is not. Learning to enjoy good wine is no more complicated than learning to enjoy good food.

The study of wine is the study of an art. Enology is not an exact science like mathematics, physics or chemistry. In math $1+1$ always equals 2. In enology one grape + one grape seldom produces an identical product. The variables of grape, soil, weather and winemaking techniques are virtually infinite. There are about 5,000 species of wine grapes (vitis vinifera), not to mention the numerous native American grapes (vitis labrusca) and the ever increasing number of French hybrid grapes. The soil producing the grapes may contain chalk, gravel, slate or other materials and varying amounts of minerals such as cobalt, copper, nickel, zinc, etc. Because of these variables, two adjacent vineyards, one across the road from the other, may produce distinctively different wines from the same grapes. The grape itself has not yet been fully analyzed by the scientists, but is known to have over 300 components. Fortunately, you do not have to study the chemical composition of wine to enjoy it. However, some comprehension of its complexity will lead to a fuller appreciation of its subleties and nuances of flavor. Just as you may learn a little about the paintings of the great masters by going to museums and drinking in famous art works, you may learn a little about wine by drinking it. Both are sensory pleasures, one for the eye, the other for the palate. But you can really learn very little about either without guidance. You might not recognize nor appreciate a Van Gogh in an art gallery unless you had studied his style and techniques and seen photographs of his works in an art book. Likewise, you might not recognize nor appreciate a Chateau Lafite Rothschild unless you read about it and knew what to look for in its color, aroma, bouquet, and taste.

Although this book will furnish you with basic wine knowledge, there are other numerous useful sources of wine information, including magazines, wine letters, importers, wineries, distributors, trade commissions, wine merchants, and other wine buffs. These sources will expand your knowledge and keep you current and aware of new developments and theories.

Magazines—Wine Letters. There are many wine periodicals available to those who wish to keep abreast of the latest news and current developments in the world of wine. Wine magazines will report on the latest vintage information, the results of wine tastings and wine evaluations, interviews with experts, the changing trends in the growing and processing of wine and winery visits by the writers. The letters to the editors are especially helpful to the neophyte because the questions posed by the letter writers are often the same questions you would have asked and the editors' replies supply the answers. Recent years have seen the development of publications known as wine letters or wine guides, which report on new developments, wine "buys," and tastings. Some of these are excellent; some are mediocre.

However, most are useful and informative because of the wide variety of subjects and the various viewpoints expressed by the authors.

Anyone seriously interested in the study of wine should subscribe to at least one wine periodical. Appendix A has a list of many of the wine magazines and wine guides currently published and where to order them.

The Trade. There is also a plethora of free wine information available from many importers, vineyards and distributors. Many of them publish and disseminate monthly newsletters, brochures, or other literature without charge. Of course, most of this material is promotional for the product the firm is selling. Nevertheless, much of it is of a general nature, informative, and enlightening. Many of them will discuss the quality of current vintages of the wines from their region or country. Often there will be comments about old and new processes for winemaking and the continual experimentation being conducted.

All you have to do is write them and ask them to place you on their mailing list. Appendix B contains a list of many of those to whom you may write for these publications.

Trade Commissions. Every major wine producing country has an organization for the promotion of its wines. These organizations will supply you, usually without charge, with such wine paraphernalia as maps of their wine regions, vintage charts, and brochures extolling the virtues of their country's wine. Their literature is extremely useful and informative. It will describe the wines produced and explain their wine control laws, how to read their labels, how their wines are classified, what grapes are used in the production of the various wines, their methods of vinification, production, volume, availability in the United States, etc. They often sponsor group tours to the wine areas of their country at very attractive group rates. A letter of inquiry about their wines will usually bring a prompt response. Appendix C lists the names and addresses of the wine promotion organizations of each major wine producing country.

Winery Visits. Personal visits to wineries can be very instructive as well as enjoyable. Most wineries are pleased to have you visit them. Most have tasting rooms where you may taste a number of their wines without charge. Many offer conducted tours of the winery and vineyards. Winery people are among the most gregarious in the world. They love to talk about wine and are sincerely interested in your honest opinion about their wines. (See Chapter 9.) Not only is a winery visit a delightful and economical way to spend a few hours, but it will give you a better understanding and appreciation of wine.

With a simple letter or telephone call, you can usually arrange to visit almost any winery in the world. The foreign trade commissions listed in Appendix C or tourists offices will be very helpful in helping you arrange visits to foreign wineries if you are fortunate enough to have the opportunity to travel abroad.

Wine Merchants. Another excellent source of wine information is your local wine merchant. All large cities have a number of honest, capable, knowledgeable wine merchants, who know the best vineyards, vintages, and shippers throughout the world. They will be glad to assist you in selecting your wines and to advise you of what to purchase. As a matter of their own best self-interest, most wine merchants will not try to unload on you an inferior or over-priced wine. They know that wine buffs are good customers and will be regular customers if they treat you fairly. This will be especially true if you deal regularly with the same one or two merchants. Such merchants will very quickly learn your personal likes and dislikes as well as your financial limitations. They will honestly discuss with you the merit or lack of merit of one wine as opposed to another. They will know what you can afford to spend and will sell you the best wine within your budget. However, be wary of the local liquor store merchant who has a very limited wine selection and tries to sell you a "bargain wine" at $.99 a bottle. A "bargain wine" is seldom a bargain. It will usually turn out to be expensive wine vinegar.

Other Wine Buffs. Tasting and discussing wine with other

wine buffs is extremely helpful, pleasant, and an easy way to expand your knowledge of wine. By joining a wine club or organizing your own, you will meet regularly with other wine buffs. (See Chapter 8.) You will never meet a wine buff who is not dying to tell you about the great new wine he recently tasted. Whether you agree or disagree is not important. (Although, he will be much happier if you agree.) He is like the explorer who has discovered a new continent, because he has tasted a wine that no one else in the world (or, at least, in the world of his friends and associates) has tasted. You can, and undoubtedly will, do the same when you become a true wine buff.

Books. If, after reading this book, your appetite for learning more has been whetted, you may wish to explore this fascinating subject in greater depth. No single volume can teach you all there is to know about wine, any more than one book can teach you all there is to know about medicine. Hundreds of books have been written about the complex subject of wine. What other books are available? What should you buy? Appendix D is a list of the books which will constitute a basic wine library plus a bibliography of other books published. Especially recommended for further study is Hugh Johnson's book, *Wine*. Mr. Johnson writes in an easy flowing, delightfully engaging style. It is one of the most readable as well as authoritative and comprehensive texts on wines of the world.

Many of the books in the bibliography contain materials on service of wine, storage of wine, wine tasting, vintages, wine and health or wine and food combinations. These subjects are addressed in detail in the chapters which follow. You may find that some of the conclusions or suggestions are at variance with the opinions expressed in some of the books listed. As with any art, opinions will vary. This is one of the great challenges of enology. No one can say that you are wrong in your appraisal of a certain wine or what wine goes with what food. Opinions will even vary in such matters as storage temperatures and the "proper" manner of service of wine. Such opinions are a matter of individual preference or experience. Right and wrong are irrelevant to such opinions. Your library is merely a guide to assist you in arriving at independent, intelligent conclusions.

Why Bother?

One may well ask, "Why should I make wine my hobby? Is it really worth all the effort?" One of the main reasons for any hobby is that it offers a complete diversion from the daily hum-drum work routine. The hobby of wine has many advantages over other hobbies. It is a lot less strenuous than jogging; and it's unlikely that you will ever pull a muscle, sprain an ankle or get hit by a car during a wine tasting. The hobby of wine requires only a few steps to the wine cellar to select today's bottle. It is not seasonal. Wine can be enjoyed any time of the day or night, rain or shine, or any time of the year. Unlike tennis or golf, it is not necessary to call in advance to reserve a court or starting time.

The study of wine offers an intellectual challenge because history and geography are an integral part of enology. The history of wine is intertwined with the history of civilization; and archeologists have traced the making of wine back at least to ancient Egypt and Persia and from there to ancient Greece and Rome. The old and new testaments of the Bible are replete with references to wine. The study of the wine regions of the wine producing countries develops a better understanding of geography. Much is learned about the topography and climatic conditions of each of the wine growing areas. The wine making technology and the wine drinking habits of the people of an area often reveal much about their character.

Besides collecting wine, many wine buffs have started making their own. The relaxation of federal and state laws on wine making has resulted in the increased popularity of amateur wine making. There are wine-making kits available in stores all over the country, and many wineries are selling grapes or grape juice for wine making. The American Wine Society boasts many amateur wine makers among its members and has available many useful publications for them.

Public interest in wine is growing by leaps and bounds. The consumption of wine in America has more than doubled in the past decade. Millions of Americans are now drinking a glass of white wine before dinner instead of a cocktail. They are finding that wine is an effective, mild tranquilizer, without the resultant mule kick of the cocktail. Unlike the cocktail, wine adds to rather than detracts from the enjoyment of the food to follow. The owner of Antoine's Restaurant in New Orleans, Roy Louis Alciatore has said:

> "Don't make the mistake of ordering a good meal and then expect to enjoy it with ice water as a beverage. A rich meal without wine is like an expensive automobile equipped with hard rubber tires. The whole effect is lost for the lack of suitable accompaniment. Rich and heavy foods that are unpalatable with water can only be appreciated with a suitable wine. Wine warms the stomach and hastens the digestion."

A knowledge of wine is considered as important a social grace as knowing what fork or spoon to use. As well as complementing the taste of the food, a decanter of wine adds beauty and charm to the dinner table. It is the catalyst which stimulates the conversation at any dinner party.

There is a cameraderie among enophiles which unites the expert and the novice. The winery owner, the wine maker, the merchant, the tasting expert, and the wine buff have a common bond; all enjoy a good glass of wine. The wine buff will seldom, if ever, be ill at ease or uncomfortable in the company of wine people, whether in America or abroad. The sharing of the first glass of wine germinates the seed of friendship and the second glass nurtures it.

The hobby of wine offers sensory pleasures not afforded by any other with the possible exception of gourmet cooking. But wine drinking does not require the washing of dirty pots and pans. I have heard of coin collectors biting a coin to test its authenticity; but I have never heard anyone say it tasted good. The sensory pleasure of wine can be enjoyed at any age. Physical infirmities will make the athletic hobbies impossible; dentures may make it difficult to enjoy a steak or an ear of corn; but the senses of taste and smell are seldom affected by old age. A glass of wine can be appreciated as much at age 90 as it can at age 25. Because of the limited sensory pleasures remaining at age 90, and because of the many years of tasting experience, wine will be more appreciated and enjoyed at age 90. Ernest Hemingway wrote:

"Wine is one of the most civilized things in the world and one of the natural things of the world that has been brought to the greatest perfection; and it offers a greater range for enjoyment and appreciation than possibly any other purely sensory thing which may be purchased."

If food is the body of good living, wine is its soul.
                                                    Clifton Fadiman

2

What Wine
With What Food?

Wine and food have a natural affinity; each complements and enhances the taste and enjoyment of the other. For centuries Europeans have been drinking wine with their meals. Perhaps this came about because in the past wine was safer to drink than water. But, in any event, for them drinking wine with their everyday dinner is the most normal, unpretentious act in the world, performed without formality or affectation. They simply open the bottle, put it on the table, drink it, and enjoy it.

But many Americans have a fear of serving wine to their dinner guests or ordering wine in a restaurant. They are afraid that they will be embarrassed or look foolish if they serve or order the wrong wine. They seem to think there is some deep, dark mystery revealed only to the chosen few, as to what wine goes with what food. Nothing could be further from the truth. There should be no more concern or anxiety about serving or ordering wine than there is about serving or ordering dinner.

There are no ironclad rules to govern wine choice, other than common sense. Of course, certain types of wines do go better with some foods than others. There are some wine-food combinations that the experience of experts has demonstrated to be excellent marriages and certainly their experience should not be completely ignored. One of the best known and most traditional wine-food combinations is Chablis and oysters. However, this does not mean that no other wine should be drunk with oysters. Many white wines such as Muscadet or Chenin Blanc are also superb complements to oysters.

The wine snob insists that certain wine-food combinations must be adhered to as if they were rules carved in granite. This is nonsense. On the other hand, there are those who might be called "reverse snobs." They are even greater bores than the snobs. These are the people who say "drink whatever wine you like with whatever food you like." As with any generality, this statement must be tempered with common sense and the experience of the experts. Certainly, Chateau Lafite-Rothschild is a superb wine; but it would be sheer foolishness to drink it at a picnic. This would be as absurd as a Chateau d'Yquem (a very sweet, white wine) with spaghetti and tomato sauce. Such combinations would be comparable to putting ketchup on strawberry shortcake.

The cliché of "red wine with red meat and white wine with white meat or fish" is another generality which one repeatedly hears. Although there is an element of truth in this statement, it is misleading because it overemphasizes color. The color of the wine or the meat is relatively inconsequential. Wines and foods should be paired according to the characteristics of each. This principle is best explained by the following examples: light, red, white or rosé wines go with light foods such as cold meats or fowl or picnic lunches. Drink heavy, rich, full-bodied red wines with heavy, rich, spicy foods such as charcoal-broiled steak or lasagna. Delicate, fine red wines complement delicate fine foods such as rack of lamb or plain broiled sirloin steaks (without sauce). Delicate, fine white wines should accompany delicate, fine foods such as brook trout or filet of flounder. Sweet wines, red or white, should be drunk with sweet foods such as cake or pastries or by themselves without food.

These guidelines make it obvious that the sauces, the condiments, the quality of the food, and the manner of preparation are the important factors in determining what wine to serve with what food. A fine red Bordeaux wine will complement a roast beef but not if a rich, spicy gravy is served with it. The gravy will overpower the fine wine. Likewise, if your picnic lunch contains spicy salami or sausages, a light white wine will be overpowered by the food and a light or medium-bodied red wine would be more appropriate. The food and the wine should blend together in a symphony of harmonizing tastes and flavors. Simple wines complement simple foods, and complex wines complement complex foods.

Many wine writers, especially those writing about European wines, suggest that certain wines are great with game or cheese or exotic foods. Their recommendations are valid and, perhaps, useful if you happen to be a hunter. However, when was the last time you ate wild boar? If you have not toured Europe, you may never have had a cheese course with your meal; and suggestions as to wine and cheese combinations may be of little practical value. The following is a listing of some of the most common American foods and the wines which will complement them.

Beef. Most Americans are meat and potato eaters; and the favorite meat is beef. American beef dishes can run the gamut from hamburger or stew to prime ribs or steak. Any dry California red jug wine will go well with a hamburger on a bun. With a Salisbury steak (hamburger on a platter), try a California Gamay Beaujolais, a non-premium Zinfandel, a Bardolino, or Valpolicella. With a rich or spicy stew, serve a Cotes du Rhone or a California Petite Sirah or Barbera, all of which are heavy wines and can stand up to the stew. With your expensive cuts of beef such as the prime ribs or steak, serve your finest wines. All of the premium red wines such as a California Cabernet Sauvignon or Zinfandel, or a chateau bottled Bordeaux, a fine French Burgundy or Chianti Classico Riserva are excellent complements to these favorite American dishes. If the steak is charcoal-broiled, a more robust wine is needed to compete with the heavy charcoal flavor. Some of the excellent Italian wines such as Gattinara or Barolo or the Spanish Riojas are rich enough to hold their own against the charcoal flavor. Most good white wines are too light, soft, and fruity to serve with beef.

Pork. Pork dishes are a different matter and white or red wine may accompany them. With a roast pork, try the French reds of Beaujolais or a regional Bordeaux or the California or German whites produced from the Riesling or Gewurtztraminer grapes or a white Spanish Rioja. With pork chops, the Italian Valpolicella or Soave or an Alsatian white will go well. A young Italian Chianti or champagne or other sparkling white wine may be served with smoked ham.

Lamb. A rack of lamb or thick lambchops without a mint or heavy sauce require the best red wines such as a fine Bordeaux, Chianti Classico Riserva or premium California Cabernet Sauvignon. Lamb stew or roast lamb with a mint or a rich sauce should be served with lesser wines such as a California Claret, Burgundy, or non-premium Zinfandel.

Veal. Red or white wines are appropriate with veal dishes depending upon the manner of preparation. The light, delicate veal dishes such as veal piccata or Florentine are best with light white wines like a California Pinot Blanc, Italian Soave or Orvieto or Alsatian Sylvaner. On the other hand, veal Parmigiana with its tomato sauce and cheese needs a red wine with body; e.g. Cotes du Rhone, Barbera or Chianti. Roast veal or plain veal cutlet give you a choice of light reds like Valpolicella or a regional Bordeaux or whites such as a German Kabinett Rhine or Mosel or California Chardonnay or Riesling.

Fowl. Chicken, turkey, and duck also offer wide latitude for the selection of wine accompaniments. Chicken is especially versatile. Almost any dry or medium dry white (Frascati, Verdicchio, Liebfraumilch, Riesling, etc.) or light red (regional Bordeaux, Valpolicella, Beaujolais, Bardolino, etc.) will be suitable with roasted, fried, or stewed chicken. Chicken à la king is best with such white wines as Vinho Verde or Orvieto or those of the Loire Valley. Because of the spiciness of the stuffing and the marked difference between the white meat and dark meat, the usual holiday turkey should be served with both a red, e.g. Chateauneuf du Pape or California Petite Sirah, and a white wine, e.g. German or California Riesling. Roast duck with an orange sauce should be accompanied by a rich, sweetish, German or California white wine; without the sweet orange sauce, a red Rhone or California Petite Sirah is fine.

Pasta. Spaghetti and other Italian pasta dishes, as they are served in America, are not always at their best with Italian wines. Italian-Americans use much more tomato sauce on their pasta dishes than do the native Italians. Many of the good Italian red wines are too fine to compete with the acidic, rich tomato sauce used so copiously in America. The Portuguese Dao is inexpensive and an excellent partner for Italian-American spaghetti as are some of the California Barberas. However, the Italian white wines of Orvieto, Soave, and Verdicchio are appropriate with pasta dishes with a white sauce such as fettucini Alfredo.

Seafood. Most fish and other seafood entrees do not go well with red wines. The more bland and delicate fishes such as flounder and brook trout are best with a light Mosel, white Burgundy, or California Chardonnay. The more oily fishes like shad and mackerel go well with a white Bordeaux or white Rioja. Many Frenchmen still drink the very sweet Sauternes with rich, oily fishes. Shellfish are best complemented by Chablis or other white Burgundies, Muscadet, or California Chardonnay.

Dessert. One of the best, most popular dessert wines is sauternes; not the non-descript, ordinary American sauterne (spelled without the final s), but an authentic French sauternes (or Barsac) with its rich, velvety, sweet smoothness, unparallelled except, perhaps, by some of the very expensive, great German sweet wines. A glass of sauternes is a luscious complement to a simple white cake, custard, or cream (not ice cream) type or other light dessert. Other traditional dessert wines are Madeira, Marsala, cream sherry, and port which go well with nuts, dried fruits, or the rich heavy desserts. A wine only recently beginning to find its way into the United States is the Italian Vin Santo, an excellent dessert wine, which goes well with almond or other nut-flavored cookies or desserts. With fresh fruits (other than citrus), try a Vouvray or medium sweet champagne or Asti Spumante.

After Dinner. All of the dessert wines are also excellent after dinner drinks and are rich, sweet, and satisfying enough to be substituted for the dessert course if you are watching your calories. A glass of Malmsey Madeira sipped with your after dinner coffee is a pleasant combination. Of course, a fine brandy, cognac, or Armagnac (distilled wine) is always appropriate as an after dinner drink.

The foregoing suggestions are by no means all inclusive either as to the wines or the foods, but are simply basic guidelines. There are innumerable other appropriate wines which may be served with each of the above foods. The suggested examples are a starting point for your own experimentation. In the final analysis, wine-food combinations come down to a matter of personal, subjective taste.

The omission of rosé wines from the suggested wine food combinations was not an oversight. Although you have probably heard it said that rosé wine goes with any food, serious wine drinkers consider most rosés inappropriate with any meal other than a light lunch or picnic. With a few exceptions, notably the French Tavel or some of the Italian dry rosé wines, the rosés are too sweet and light to complement fine foods. The often-made comment that rosé wines are for people who don't like wine is an overstatement of the case against rosés. With a sandwich of tuna fish, American cheese, chicken salad, or some similar light lunch, a cool glass of rosé wine can be very pleasant. Certainly, well-chilled rosé is a refreshing beverage for a hot summer afternoon as a substitute for a cold beer or cola, but is totally unsuitable as an accompaniment to prime beef or rack of lamb.

Just as rosés are especially drinkable in warm or hot weather, likewise the selection of many of the wine-food combinations are also influenced by the season of the year. This is particularly true of red wines. As indicated, there are numerous wines which are fitting complements to beef depending upon the cut or manner of preparation. Although a Barolo is delicious with a charcoal-broiled steak in cold weather, in mid-summer with its 85° temperatures, you may find the lighter and slightly chilled, Bardolino, Gamay, Beaujolais, or Valpolicella more pleasing. Just as lighter foods are often eaten during the dog days of summer, similarly lighter red wines are more enjoyable than the heavy reds.

The purist will advise that if you are going to have a good bottle of wine with dinner, the cocktails should be omitted. He would recommend the traditional cocktail Sherry, either the dry Fino or the slightly sweet Amontillado, or champagne or a sparkling wine or almost any dry or medium dry white wine. If you are having a simple one or two course meal with an ordinary everyday wine, it is appropriate to have a glass of your dinner wine as an aperitif. Or, in place of the cocktail, substitute a dry vermouth, well chilled or even on the rocks.

However, unless one has an extremely low tolerance for alcohol, one dry martini or manhattan will not affect the enjoyment or appreciation of wine. Many wine authorities will disagree with this conclusion, which is based on the writer's personal experience and observation. The alcoholic content of a three ounce dry martini and a three ounce glass of sherry are not substantially different. Gin is usually 80 to 90 proof (40% to 45% alcohol). Sherry is about 40 proof (20% alcohol). The three ounce dry martini is only about one and a half ounces of gin, and a dash of vermouth, the remaining one and a half ounces being water from mixing the gin with ice. Thus, the gin is diluted approximately 50% to about 40 proof, the same as the proof and the volume of alcohol in the three ounces of sherry. Of course, three or four cocktails before dinner are not recommended. The total enjoyment of a fine wine requires that one be in full control of his faculties and that his senses not be dulled by over-indulgence. If you are flying high from three generous dry martinis, you probably will not appreciate the delicacy, nuances of taste and finesse of a fine wine. As with most things in life, moderation is dictated. Let common sense and your own experience be your guide.

There are few foods (fortunately, only a few) which simply do not blend with any wine. Vinegar is one of these. Thus, America's "Italian" dressing will devastate the taste of any wine. The vinegar residue in the mouth will turn the entire mouthful of wine into vinegar. Chocolate is also anathema to wine. No wine should be drunk with a chocolate dessert which will destroy the flavor of the wine. Ice cream and wine do not go together. The acid of citrus fruits will also overpower the wine. In all of these cases, the food does nothing for the wine, and the wine does nothing for the food.

Don't adhere to oversimplified slogans or clichés of wine drinking. Don't be a wine snob; but don't over-react and drink any wine with any food. Be adventurous, but reasonable, in trying various wines with different foods. When taste and common sense lead the way, the opportunity for experimentation with palate-teasing wine-food combinations are virtually infinite.

3

Wine Service

Service of everyday wine requires no special preparation or planning. First, remove the foil (or often today, plastic) from around the top of the bottle. It is not unusual to find mold or dirt under the foil capsule. This should be of no concern because it does not in any way affect the wine. The mold or dirt should be wiped clean with a damp cloth or paper towel before attacking the cork.

Modern corkscrews simplify the problem of removing the cork. The better corkscrews work on leverage principles and are very effective. Figure 1 pictures three popular corkscrews, all of which are very satisfactory and efficient. After the cork is removed, again wipe the neck of the bottle, inside and out, to avoid contamination of the wine from any residual mold or dirt. Occasionally, a cork is stubborn or defective and will break in half leaving part of the cork in the neck of the bottle. If this happens, remove the broken section, and reinsert the corkscrew

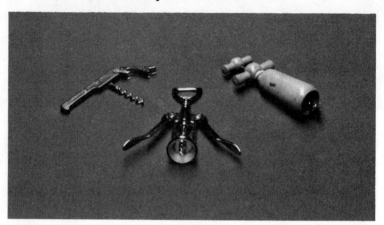

Figure 1

into the remaining half. Sometimes the reinsertion of the cork-screw will push the remaining half of the cork back into the bottle, and it will be impossible to remove it. This is no great catastrophe. Simply decant the wine and serve it from the decanter after you have removed any cork particles floating in the wine.

A bottle of champagne or sparkling wine requires special treatment. It is usually stoppered with a mushroom-like cork or plastic cap. After removing the foil and wire around the neck of the bottle, gently twist the protruding knob, at the same time lifting it slightly. After one or two turns, you will feel the pressure of the gas in the bottle pushing on the cork. Allow the pressure to take over and slowly expel the cork. As the pressure starts pushing out the cork, you may even find that you have to exert counter-pressure to keep the cork from flying out of the bottle. There should be only the slightest "pop" when the cork is removed, not the "big bang" so often associated with opening champagne. The wine should not bubble out. If the champagne froths out of the bottle, too much of the gas escapes and the wine will go flat quicker; and even worse, a lot of expensive wine will have been wasted.

Decanting of still wines is generally advisable. Decanting means to pour the wine from the bottle into another container, which may be a fine crystal decanter or a plain wide mouth carafe, such as that used in many restaurants to serve their house wines. There is something esthetically pleasing about a decanter or carafe on the dining table; a brilliant red wine in a sparkling crystal decanter adds color and vibrancy to any table. Decanting also allows the wine to "breathe," releasing the volatile esters and aldehydes which give the wine its aroma and bouquet and stimulate the olfactory senses. The finer the wine, the more complex will be its aroma and bouquet, which together are often referred to as the "nose" of the wine.

In recent years an interesting controversy has developed in the wine world concerning the necessity of allowing wine to breathe. For generations there was complete agreement among wine experts that all red wines should be opened at least one-half hour to three hours before serving to allow the air to react upon the wine. In May 1977, Alexis Bespaloff shook the foundations of the wine establishment with an article concluding that breathing does not improve red wine, and in many cases, is detrimental. Everyone agrees that white or rosé wines do not require breathing time.

With one exception, I agree with the old school of thought that good red wines require decanting and ample breathing time. I have found that many California reds lose some of their better qualities and develop a "grassy" taste after being open for more than a half-hour. Most good French wines and many of the better California reds will improve with one-half hour to two hours of breathing time. The heavier the wine, the more breathing is required. Most of the Italian, Spanish, and Portuguese red wines are at their best after a minimum of two hours of breathing time. Generally, younger wines should be allowed to breathe longer than older wines. Since many of the experts will disagree on the issue of breathing, you should experiment and arrive at your own conclusions.

Few people have not heard the rule that red wine should be drunk at room temperature; but many fail to understand the meaning of the term, "room temperature." (I have heard innu-

merable people say "I don't like warm wine." Neither do I!)
Room temperature does not mean the temperature of the average overheated home or apartment. It means about 65° to 70°
Fahrenheit. No wine should be drunk at a temperature over 70°.
White wines are best served at about 45° to 50°. This can be
accomplished by putting the white wine in the refrigerator for
about one hour prior to serving it, or the unopened bottle can
also be placed in a bucket of ice for twenty minutes to a half
hour. The ice bucket should be deep enough to allow the ice to
reach the neck of the bottle. The wine will chill quicker if water
is added to the ice and if you occasionally rotate the bottle and
even turn it upside down for a few minutes to chill the neck of
the bottle. The finer the wine, the higher the temperature at
which it should be drunk within the foregoing limits. A Beaujolais or Bardolino may well be served slightly chilled or at cellar
temperature of about 55°. A fine Bordeaux or California Cabernet Sauvignon may taste best at 68°. A California jug white wine
labelled Chablis is fine at 40°; but a good white Burgundy like a
Mersault may taste best at 60°. Personal preference is the most
important factor in determining at what temperature a particular
wine should be served.

Although the service of everyday wines is uncomplicated, the
service of fine, aged red wines does require some minimal preparation and planning beforehand. A twenty-year-old Bordeaux,
Barolo, or vintage Port will "throw" a heavy sediment in the
bottle. Since the wine has been stored "laying down," this sediment will accumulate along the bottom side of the bottle. Therefore, if it is opened and poured immediately, much of the sediment will be poured into the glass or decanter. Such a wine
should be stood upright for at least twenty-four hours before
pulling the cork, in order to allow the sediment to settle into the
punt (the indentation) in the bottom of the bottle. Care must be
taken not to shake or disturb the sediment when transporting
the bottle from the cellar. If the bottle is shaken, the sediment
will be dispersed throughout the wine causing it to become
cloudy and muddy.

The sediment in wine consists of mostly tannins which impart
the astringent taste to the wine and are an integral substance of

all red wines. The tannins are derived from the skins, pips, and stems of the grape. Shaking or disturbing the sediment not only makes the wine cloudy and detracts esthetically from its color, but also distributes the tannins throughout the wine making it bitter. Since white wines are not fermented with the skins, pips, or stems, they have little or no tannin and do not usually throw a sediment. However, a crystalline deposit, looking like small slivers of glass, may sometimes be found in the bottom of the bottle or on the cork of white wine and even occasionally of reds. These crystals are tartrates, completely harmless and taste-less, and, therefore, do not affect the wine. But, again, for esthetic reasons, the wine should be decanted to eliminate the crystals.

To avoid getting the sediment or crystals in the decanter, the decanting process must be carefully performed. It must be done slowly in one continuous motion in front of a light in order that the sediment may be observed as the wine is poured. The classic way of decanting a wine is with the use of a lighted candle which is placed just behind the neck of the bottle. (Any bright light, even a flashlight, will do.) As the wine is poured, the light of the candle shines through the bottle neck and shoulder allowing visual observation of the sediment as it approaches the neck of the bottle. As soon as the sediment reaches the neck of the bottle, the pouring is stopped and only the crystal clear wine enters the decanter.

Glasses

All the effort of bringing the wine up or down to the right tem-perature, removing the cork and decanting it, can be an exercise in futility if the wine is served in an unsuitable glass. This does not mean that each type of wine must be served in its own style of glass. It simply means that the wine should be served in a true wine glass. Until the late 19th century, colored glasses were often used to cover up the cloudiness of the wines which did not have the benefit of modern fining and clarification processes. Today, a colored wine glass is considered completely unaccept-able. A wine glass should be clear, colorless, and thin. It should be large, at least eight ounces and preferably ten ounces or more. The glass should be stemmed and the bowl should be smaller at the top than in the middle.

A proper glass is not an affectation; it is very functional. The senses of sight and smell are essential to the full appreciation of wine. A good wine glass makes possible the use of the senses to their full advantage. A clear glass allows the observation of the color and clarity of the wine. A tinted glass would distort its true color. The glass must be large to allow room to release the aroma and bouquet by swirling the normal serving of about four ounces without having the wine slosh over the sides. The shape of the bowl helps to confine the aroma and bouquet within the glass; and the glass is large enough that even a Cyrano could get his nose into it to smell the wine. The long stem serves the utilitarian purpose of keeping the heat of the hand from warming the wine. Fine, thin crystal glasses fitting these qualifications are perfect for formal dinner parties. But for everyday use, an inexpensive tulip glass is ideal and can be washed in the dishwasher without worrying about breakage. This is an all purpose wine glass and is even suitable for champagne. (Figures 2 and 3 are the two basic tulip shaped styles.)

Champagne should never be served in the popular champagne glass used for the toast at every wedding reception. This is the glass which Hugh Johnson has so aptly dubbed "a saucer on a stem." No good sparkling wine is inexpensive. It is ridiculous to pay the price for all those beautiful bubbles only to have them dissipate into the air almost as quickly as the wine is poured. The tulip shaped glass exposes a much smaller surface of the wine to the air, and therefore, traps the bubbles in the glass for a much longer time. Another popular and appropriate glass is the Paris goblet. (See Figure 4.)

Another popular style glass is the balloon glass. This is a very large (sixteen ounces), clear, tall glass about eight inches high. Some consider it an obnoxious ostentation because of its enormous size. Similar styles are available in ten or twelve ounce sizes. (See Figure 5.)

Figure 2   Figure 3

How to Store

Wine glasses should never be stored upside down. They should always be stored upright to allow the air to circulate through the bowl and avoid the musty smell of stale air in the glass. Many kitchen or bar shelves are lined with a vinyl or plastic covering which could impart a foreign odor to the wine. A speck or two of dust is far more tolerable in the wine than the smell of stale air or plastic.

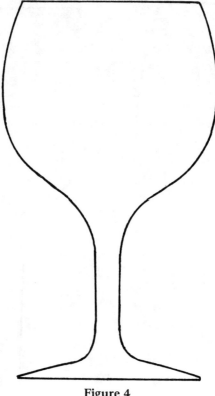

Figure 4

How to Serve

There are three general rules about the order of serving wines if you are having more than one. Dry wines are served before sweet, just as you serve the entreé before the dessert. White wines should precede reds because most whites lack the intensity and depth of flavor of reds. If the red is drunk first, it may be so overpowering that by comparison, even a fine white may taste flat and bland. For the same reason, young wines should be served before old. As with most "rules" of wine ritual, there are exceptions; and the overriding rule is to complement the food

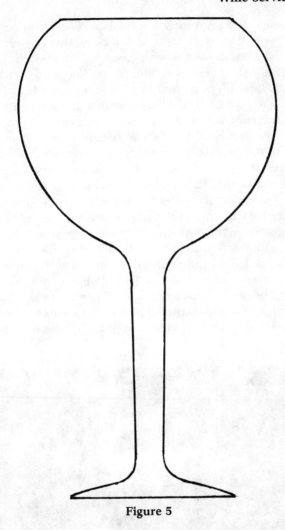

Figure 5

with the wine. There are some foods, such as smoked salmon or an oily fish, served at an early course of a dinner which may be more appropriate with a sweet rather than a dry white wine. In such event, the food wine combination is the primary consideration and the foregoing rules are secondary.

Traditionally, the host serves a small portion, an ounce or so, of the wine to himself to taste. Historically, this custom relates back to the Middle Ages when a guest had to concern himself about getting an undesired potion of poison in his wine. The host would taste the wine first to assure the guest of the potability of the wine. Today it is still done so that the host will be satisfied that the wine is not bad and is fit to serve to his guests. Of course, if the host has decanted and tasted the wine in advance, this step in the ritual is unnecessary. After tasting the wine, the host serves the guests around the table clockwise. Some say serve the ladies first then go around the table again and serve the men. Others say it is proper to serve the men and women in one clockwise trip around the table or even to have the guests pass the glasses to the host who fills them (never more than one-half full) and passes them back. Then the host fills his glass. If there is wine left in the bottle, the bottle may remain on the table on a wine coaster or in a cooler for white wines to the right of the host or on a sideboard. (Figure 6 demonstrates three different styles of wine coasters.) If the host walks around the table, the wine should be served from the right side, since the

Figure 6

Figure 7

wine glasses are placed to the right of the guest's plate. Of course, the cardinal rule is to use common sense and serve the wine in the most convenient and appropriate manner under all the circumstances.

Wrapping a napkin around the bottle is a useless ostentation, unless you are ashamed of the wine and wish to hide the label from the guests. A napkin may be useful to wipe dry a bottle of white wine after pulling it from the cooler or ice bucket to avoid dripping water over the guests or to wipe the neck of the bottle to avoid the dripping of the wine. However, a twist of the wrist as each glass is filled will usually prevent the wine from dripping from the bottle. There is one utilitarian reason for wrapping a champagne bottle with a napkin. It is possible, although remote, that the heat of the hand on the cold bottle when the cork is being pulled may cause the carbon dioxide gas inside to expand and the bottle to burst. The napkin offers some protection against this possibility because it insulates the cold bottle from the warm hand. However, once the cork is removed, the napkin should be removed.

A wine cradle (Figure 7) serves no functional purpose whatsoever and may even be detrimental to the proper service of wine.

The Burgundians invented the wine cradle for the purpose of carrying the wine from the cellar in the same horizontal position in which it is binned to avoid disturbing the sediment. Since any wine with substantial sediment should stand upright for a day or two before decanting to allow the sediment to collect in the punt, the use of a wine cradle defeats this purpose because tilting the bottle back on its side again stirs up the sediment.

4

Guests and Wine

Now that you are a confirmed wine buff, the cliché, "a dinner without wine is like a day without sunshine," has real meaning for you. You would not think of sitting down to a good meal without a bottle of wine. You drink wine with dinner every evening or at least two or three times a week and certainly on all special occasions. You are hooked!

One of the great pleasures for the wine buff is sharing a fine bottle of wine with a friend. Wine is a social drink, and the sheer ecstasy of an exceptional bottle cannot be fully enjoyed and appreciated alone. Even a modest wine will taste better in the company of others. Without a companion to talk about it, most of the enjoyment of drinking a fine wine is lost.

But, most of your friends will have varying degrees of interest in and knowledge of wine. What wine should you serve to your friends when they are dining in your home? This is not a simple question for the neophyte to answer. It becomes less difficult with experience as your own personal preferences develop. You must first decide what food you are going to serve (for food-wine combinations see chapter 2) and how much you can afford to spend for the wine. Only you and your pocketbook can resolve what you can afford.

After establishing the menu and determining how much you wish to spend, the ultimate decision of what wine to serve will depend upon your guests. You must know whether or not your guests like wine, their degree of wine sophistication, and into what category they fit.

Guest Classifications

You may classify your dinner guests into five categories:

1. The *Unfortunates:* those who "don't like wine."

2. The *Dogmatists:* those who say "I know what wine I like, you can keep the others."

3. The *Unsophisticates:* those who like wine but admit "I don't know a thing about it."

4. The *Snobs:* those who think they know something about wine but have only a superficial knowledge or may be knowledgeable about French wines but think all others are grossly inferior.

5. The *Sophisticates:* those who are truly experts, connoisseurs, and dedicated, knowledgeable wine buffs.

The Unfortunates. You must feel sorry for this group. The education of their palate to one of life's epicurean delights has been woefully neglected. It is almost impossible to believe that there is not some wine that they will like. Stating "I don't like wine" is like saying "I don't like ethnic food." One may not like crepes or calalmari or sauerbraten or ham and cabbage. But, it does not follow that he will not like quiche or bacala or wiener schnitzel or Irish stew. All are ethnic dishes. But there is such a wide variety of ethnic foods to choose from that only a food fanatic or faddist could say "I don't like any of them." So it is with wine. When a guest says that he doesn't like wine, you may conclude that his previous experience has been confined to cheap, tart French or Italian "bargain" wines, which have convinced him that all wines taste the same. He is obviously unaware that wines can run the gamut from very dry to syrupy sweet, from very light to very heavy, from colorless to black, from bland to spicy. The nuances of aroma, bouquet, texture, and taste are virtually infinite. There is a wine or wines to suit the taste of everyone.

The Dogmatists. The Dogmatist always drinks the same one or the same few wines or types of wines. He is the unimaginative fellow who always orders a steak in a restaurant (and probably smothers it with ketchup) ignoring the multitude of other taste sensations available. He has discovered a wine that he likes and always drinks the same one. He is often the same person who will try to convince you that the cherry sweet Portuguese rosés are the epitome of wine appreciation. He refuses to experiment with food or wine. He is doomed to an epicurean life of dullness and boredom but, fortunately for him, does not know it.

The Unsophisticates. The Unsophisticates are diametric opposites of the Dogmatists. The Unsophisticate acknowledges his ignorance but is usually willing, often eager, to try a different wine. He has an open mind and is happy to experiment. He will try to be objective and has no preconceived prejudices. Although, as a guest, he may present the greatest challenge in selection of a wine, he will also offer the greatest satisfaction if you are fortunate enough to select a wine he likes. The Unsophisticate affords you the opportunity of exposing his taste buds to a revelation of gustatory experience. He may be almost ecstatic about his newfound sensual pleasure and overwhelm you with his expressions of gratitude.

The Snobs. The Snob is closely related to the Dogmatist, although he is usually more knowledgeable. Nevertheless, he is only slightly less boring than the Dogmatist. For some inexplicable reason, wine snobs are French wine addicts. One never hears of an Italian or Australian or Chilean wine snob. Somehow the snob has been brainwashed to believe that if a wine is not

French it is inferior; and if it is French, it must be good. The typical snob in his arrogance refuses to acknowledge the merit of any wine except for a chateau-bottled Bordeaux or a Tête de Cuvée French Burgundy. For him all other wines are inferior. He will refuse to admit that a fine California Cabernet or Italian Chianti Classico or Spanish Rioja could ever compare even to a poor vintage of Chateau Margaux or Chateau Mouton Rothschild, even though the latter may cost five times as much as the former. He is the fellow who drinks labels – not wine.

The Sophisticates. The Sophisticates are those truly knowledgeable wine experts or wine buffs who have studied and tasted wine for many years and have an objective appreciation of all good, sound wines, regardless of the place of origin or the price. The Sophisticate is the category of guest with whom you can enjoy any wine whether it be very modest or very fine. He will be appreciative of your efforts at selection even though he may disagree with you. He will share his knowledge with you and respect your opinion. He recognizes the Latin adage *De gustibus non est disputandum.* (Concerning tastes, there is no dispute.)

What Wines to Serve

The Unfortunates and the Dogmatists will be the most difficult dinner guests to please. Although the Unfortunates will probably not be impossible, the Dogmatists may very well be. In either case, do not serve your best bottles. You cannot possibly educate them instantly to the finesse, character, delicacy, bouquet, or overtones of taste or aftertaste of a fine vintage wine. That would be like trying to teach an illiterate to read and appreciate Shakespeare in one lesson. With either of this type, you will probably be more successful with a white wine than a red wine. Have them try a Vinho Verde from Portugal or a German Mosel, such as a Crover Nachtarch or Zeller Schwarze Katz. All are light, pleasant, white wines. The Vinho Verde will often be a little "bubbly" which adds to its interest and enjoyment. The two

German wines will be slightly sweeter than the Vinho Verde. Any of them would complement a seafood dish or a light, mildly spiced meat. Satisfying guests in either of these categories with a red wine is a much more challenging task because most reds are more astringent and drier than whites. You must be wary about trying to please them with just a single red wine selection. Although you might personally prefer a good French Bordeaux, California Cabernet or Italian Chianti Classico with your dinner, you should introduce these guests to some of the modestly priced California wines which generally appeal to the American palate, such as a Gallo Hearty Burgundy or a Paul Masson or Charles Krug Gamay Beaujolais. With dessert or as an after dinner treat, try an Asti Spumante from Italy. An alternate dessert wine would be a French sauternes which is very sweet and perfectly complements a dessert of plain white cake. Do not buy an American sauterne (note the difference in spelling) if you want a dessert wine. American sauterne may be dry, semisweet, or sweet. You cannot be sure unless you have tried it. A French sauternes is always sweet. If your Dogmatist guest is a true Dogmatist, have a well-chilled bottle of rosé ready for him when he turns up his nose to the above selections. However, do not waste your money on the over-priced but popular Portuguese rosés. Serve him an Italian or California rosé and save yourself one or two dollars a bottle. If none of the foregoing suggestions please your Unfortunate or Dogmatist guest, he is hopeless. The next time invite him to lunch instead of dinner; pour him a coke and make him a bologna sandwich.

The Unsophisticates will not usually be too difficult to please. They have probably tasted many good wines and enjoyed them but never took the trouble to remember them. For these guests, serve a medium-priced good wine but not your finest. They may not be quite ready to appreciate the subtle differences between a very good wine and a great wine. However, neither should you serve them a rosé wine with a fine dinner. Their palates have likely graduated beyond the rosé class. If you plan on serving a white wine, it could be a French Muscadet or Graves or a German Kabinett Rhine or Mosel or a California Chardonnay or Italian Soave or Orvieto, all of which should be priced between

$3.00 to $5.00 per bottle. Your choice of red wine is almost unlimited. You should eliminate from consideration for this guest the inexpensive jug reds and the very fine, but usually expensive, French and California reds. In other words, the medium-priced reds at $3.00 to $6.00 per bottle would be ideal. In this price range, you can select from among such excellent wines as a Spanish Rioja, an Italian Chianti Classico, a French St. Emilion, or a Chilean Cabernet. You will find references to specific vineyards or shippers of all of these wines in chapter 10 from which you can make your selections.

Probably the most difficult (certainly, the most expensive) guests to please are the Snobs. You may be able to impress this category of dinner guest but you will probably not really please him. Make sure the Snob sees the label on the wine bottle. He will not dare to denigrate a Chateau Haut Brion or Cheval Blanc. Nevertheless, he will very likely find some real or imaginative flaw in the wine but excuse it because of the label. Unfortunately, you may not be able to afford the price of $15.00 to $35.00 (or even more depending upon the vintage) for either of these two great chateau wines. Thus, in order to avoid bankruptcy, you may be obliged to serve a more moderately priced wine. Among the whites, an almost universal favorite among Snobs is the good, but outrageously overpriced Pouilly Fuisse. Your other equally higher-priced alternatives and better wines would be a Meursault or a Grand Cru Chablis, both of which are very fine French wines. You may take a chance of impressing him with one of the excellent California Chardonnays, which unfortunately are gradually approaching the price of the French whites. Among the French reds which you may be able to afford for your Snob guest (if you brown bag your lunch for a week) are the Burgundies of Gevrey Chambertin, Pommard or Vosne Romanée or the Bordeaux of Chateau Kirwan, Pontet Canet, Cantemerle or Beychevelle. Also, because it is fashionable today, you may serve one of the special bottlings of Cabernet Sauvignon of one of the small boutique wineries of California, which may cost as much as some of the French Bordeaux or Burgundy wines. If your Snob guest has not been too oppressingly unbearable and boring, and if you are able to survive the financial shock of the cost of the wines you served, you will discover that the wines were indeed superb and look forward to drinking them again with guests who are Sophisticates.

The Sophisticates would undoubtedly enjoy any of the wines recommended for serving the Snobs. However, the Sophisticates will also be pleased by any sound, well-made wine. They will be especially pleased to drink a good wine which they have not previously tasted. They love to experiment and nothing pleases them more than finding a new wine. Thus, if you have discovered a very pleasing wine from some minor chateau of Bordeaux, or a relatively unknown Burgundy Appellation, or a little known producer of Chianti Classico Riserva, Barolo, or Gattinara, do not be afraid to share your discovery with the Sophisticates. You will find that in most cases, they will agree with your appraisal of the wine. Their agreement will result not from insincere politeness but rather from an honest appraisal of the wine. You may be surprised to learn that even your relatively inexperienced judgment will be confirmed by the Sophisticates. Most serious wine drinkers will generally agree upon the merit or lack of merit of a particular wine. Of course, there are often honest differences of opinion. Such differences merely contribute to a broader, mutual understanding. By discussing such differences or areas of agreement, as the case may be, everyone benefits from the exchange of ideas.

How Much to Serve

If you are having a dinner party where you are going to omit cocktails or spirits and where wine will be served exclusively, be careful not to underestimate the quantity of wine you will require. Just as you make certain that you have enough food for everyone, you must also make certain you have enough wine. It would be extremely embarrassing to have an inadequate amount of either. The usual bottle of wine is approximately 24 ounces (¾th of a liter). A generous glass of an apperitif, dessert wine, or any fortified wine is about two to two and one-half ounces and of a table wine about four ounces. The serving of fortified wine is normally smaller than that of a table wine because it has brandy or alcohol added to it resulting in a high alcoholic content of 18% to 20%; e.g. vermouth, sherry. Dessert wine, which may or may not be fortified with brandy or alcohol, is served in small portions because of its rich sweetness. Thus, each bottle of fortified or dessert wine will yield about ten to twelve servings and table wine about six. If your apertif wine is a fortified wine, one bottle will probably suffice for six people. This will allow each guest about two glasses before dinner. If your aperitif wine is a light white or sparkling wine, you should have an extra bottle chilled and ready to serve if needed, since each serving should be about four ounces. One bottle of dessert wine will be adequate for six people.

With dinner you can anticipate that each guest will drink two or three glasses of table wine. Therefore, for a party of six, you should have available not less than two bottles of table wine; and if your guests are also wine buffs, three bottles will not be too much. It is not unusual or excessive at a four-hour dinner party, assuming no hard liquor is served, to consume a total of one bottle of wine per person, e.g., two bottles of sparkling wine as an aperitif, three bottles of red table wine with dinner, and one bottle of sweet wine with dessert.

What to Do With Leftover Wine

Now that you are a wine buff, you will never have to buy another bottle of vinegar. You can make your own vinegar with a minimum amount of effort. All you need is a one or two quart large-mouth, glass jar with a screw cap. A mayonnaise or fruit juice jar will do fine. Pour about two inches of a good commercial red wine vinegar into the jar as a starter. Whenever you have a little leftover dry red wine, whether it is the dregs in the bottle after decanting or the leftovers in the glasses after a party, pour the leftover wine into your vinegar bottle. Let the cap sit loosely on top of the bottle to allow air to enter but prevent dust from entering. In a few short weeks the wine will turn to vinegar. The longer you leave it, the stronger the vinegar will get. Merely repeat this process with all your leftover wine and you will have a full bottle of wine vinegar in a short time. When your bottle is full, pour off about three-fourths of it through a filter into another container. An empty wine bottle will serve well as your transfer container. You can use coffee filters for filtering the vinegar. Don't worry about it if your vinegar is still a little cloudy; it won't affect its taste. The one-quarter of your vinegar which you left in the large jar is now the starter for your next batch of vinegar.

Use only dry red wine for your vinegar. You can mix leftover Bordeaux, Chianti, Rioja, California and other red wines, but do not add whites, rosés, or any sweet wines to the vinegar jar. You will find that your vinegar is much stronger than the commercial varieties you can purchase. Therefore, you should use less of it in recipes or dilute it with water to reduce its concentration.

Good company, good wine, good welcome make good people.
William Shakespeare

5

Wining and Dining Out

Don't be intimidated by a restaurant wine list and stare at it with fear and trepidation. It is really not a labyrinth designed to ensnare you in its maze of French, Italian, and German names. It is quite harmless, whether it be a simple cardboard sheet listing the wines or a pretentious, 30-page, leather- (or more likely vinyl-) bound volume. Reassure yourself with the knowledge that most people (usually including your waiter) do not know any more about the wines on the list than you.

Remember, when you dine in a good restaurant, you are there for your pleasure and enjoyment, not to accommodate the convenience or whims of your waiter or wine steward. Don't rush! Take your time. You are out to enjoy a pleasant, leisurely, relaxing couple of hours or more. Request the wine list with the menu and study both of them together, so that you may select the wine which will best complement the food you order at a price you can afford. If the waiter is solicitously hovering at your elbow, while you are perusing the menu and wine list, ask him to leave and return in ten or fifteen minutes. When he returns, order your wine. Do not order your food until the wine is delivered to your table. The waiter may think you are somewhat odd but, generally, he will indulge your idiosyncrasy. If you order your dinner before the wine, or even at the same time, the wine might arrive just in time for dessert. There are two other very good reasons for insisting that your wine be served before you order your food. First, if you have ordered a red wine, you want it opened immediately to allow it to "breathe" as long as possible before the entrée arrives. As indicated in the preceding chapter, most red wines will improve after they have been opened for at least one half hour or more. Second, if you have ordered a white or rosé wine, you want to be certain that it is adequately chilled before drinking it. A warm white or rosé wine is as limp and as dull as a warm green salad.

If none of the wines on the list appeal to you or your pocketbook, don't feel obligated to order one you don't really want or can't afford. Just because you requested to see the wine list does not mean that you have entered into an irrevocable, legally-binding contract to purchase a bottle. It is not unusual or socially unacceptable to look at the wine list and decline to order because you find nothing you like or because the prices are outrageously high.

Too often restaurant wine prices are totally unreasonable. Unfortunately, this is often especially true in some of the finer restaurants, where the price of wine may be marked up from 200% to 500% over cost. Certainly, the restaurant owner is entitled to a fair profit and a markup of 100% over wholesale cost is a fair price. A markup of 100% over retail price is high but not outrageous.

In most restaurants today, if you have a cocktail before dinner, a bottle of wine with dinner, and an after dinner brandy or liqueur, your beverage bill will exceed your food bill. There is something grossly wrong with such a system. If more consumers would revolt against paying $2.00 to $3.50 for a cocktail or brandy (the cost of which is about 35¢ to 60¢) or paying $15.00

for a bottle of wine which costs $4.00 to $6.00, restauranteurs would be obliged to stop gouging the customer. But as long as the public will pay the price, the proprietors will charge it.

There are few restaurants with good wine cellars. Even the finest restaurant in your area probably has a poor to mediocre selection of wines. For some inexplicable reason, even those restaurants which are meticulous about the quality and preparation of their food often pay little attention to their wine list. Perhaps it is from sheer stupidity or laziness or a lack of awareness of the public's expanding knowledge and interest in wine. Too often the wine list is prepared by the wholesale distributor who, naturally, "pushes" the wines he is selling, ignoring similar superior types of wine which he does not distribute. With the public's growing interest in and sophistication about wine, the restauranteur would be well advised to give the same consideration to the wine list that he gives to the menu. He should realize that most customers who appreciate fine food are often the same people who appreciate fine wine.

In many restaurants the red wines are too young and the whites and rosés are too old. It is foolish to spend $25.00 to $50.00 for a three-year-old bottle of Grand Cru Classé Bordeaux red wine which, because of its immaturity, may taste no better than a carafe of jug wine at a fraction of the price. Not only is such extravagance foolish, it is a shameful waste of what would probably be a superb wine four or five years later. Because of the poor cellar conditions of many restaurants, white wines do not mature as they should. Do not spend a lot of money for a white wine. White wines are much more volatile than the reds and poor storage conditions will adversely affect the whites quicker than the reds.

Don't be humbled by the usual wine serving ritual which, although it involves much showmanship, also serves the practical purpose of assuring the soundness of the wine. The ritual is really quite simple. The wine steward or waiter should show you the bottle before opening it. (Although, too often, the bottle is opened at the bar before being delivered to you.) This is to permit you to check the label for the type of wine and vintage year, so that you may be assured that the wine is the one you ordered before it is opened. The age at which a wine should be drunk varies greatly with the general type of wine (red, rosé, white) and the area or country of origin. Contrary to popular belief, all red wines do not improve with age. The light red wines of Beaujolais, Bardolino, and Valpolicella and most white and rosé wines are at their best between one to three years of age. The premium red wines of the world should be at least four to five years old and even much older for the truly great ones. If the wine is not precisely what you ordered or if it is too young or too old, do not hesitate to say so and request a different vintage or even a different wine.

After you acknowledge that the wine is the one you ordered, the server will open the bottle and either hand you the cork or place it on the table. He does not do this because he thinks you look like the type who collects corks. This is standard procedure. You should feel and sniff the cork, roll it between your index finger and thumb to make sure it is firm and doesn't crumble. A deteriorated cork usually indicates that too much air got into the bottle and spoiled the wine. If, when you sniff the cork, you can smell it, the wine may be bad (corky). If you smell only wine or nothing at all, the wine is probably good.

The waiter will then pour about one-half ounce of wine into your glass. Swirl it in the glass for about three seconds to release the bouquet, then, sniff the wine. You can often detect the aroma of a bad wine before you taste it. Finally, take a sip of the wine, swish it around in your mouth and swallow it. In some of the really posh restaurants, the wine steward may be bedecked in all his sommelier finery with a silver tastevin (Figure 8) around his neck. He may pour a little into the tastevin and taste it himself before pouring any into your glass. You should not be offended and think he is trying to get a free taste of your expensive wine. He merely wants to make certain the wine is good before serving it to you.

If the wine is bad, return it. "Bad" means spoiled. It does not mean that you do not like it, or that it does not appeal to you. You should know, more or less, how the wine should taste before you order it. For example, you are not justified in returning a bottle of Cabernet Sauvignon because it is too dry and you

Figure 8

prefer a wine with a tinge of sweetness, nor in returning a bottle
of French Sauternes because it is too sweet (which it should be)
and you expected a dry white wine.

It takes a lot longer to read about the wine serving ritual than
it does to perform it. After the first couple of times, you will
probably be able to participate in the ritual comfortably and
confidently without any feeling of self-consciousness, because
you know the reasons for the ritual. You will discover that you
can feel and sniff the cork and swirl, sniff, and taste the wine all
in about 10 or 15 seconds.

During dinner, the waiter or wine steward will often refill the
glasses at the table. The really solicitous server will not even
wait until a glass is drained before he refills it. I suspect that he
presumes that if he empties the bottle quickly, you may order
another which will result in a larger gratuity. I often inform the
waiter that I will pour the wine myself. I prefer doing it personally because I don't want my glass more than half full and too
many waiters insist on filling the glass to the rim. Also, I find it

annoying to have the waiter hovering over my shoulder and interfering with the conversation as he repeatedly thrusts his arm among the diners to fill the glasses.

If most restaurant wines are too young or too old or too expensive, what do you order in a restaurant? Do you forget the wine and have a bottle of beer instead? In some restaurants this may be necessary. After all, just because you are a wine buff does not mean that you will not prefer a good bottle of beer over a poor bottle of wine. However, most restaurants list a few selections which can be considered "safe" wines, ones that are reasonably priced, well-made and pleasant to drink. Although a safe wine is never a great wine, it is one which is consistent and will seldom be disappointing. Among the best are the wines of the Veneto, Italy such as Valpolicella (red) and Soave (white). Other safe wines would include Beaujolais (red) and Liebfraumilch (white). Also, many regional wines of France and Germany from good, reliable shippers (e.g. B&G, A. DeLuze & Fils, Deinhard and Kreusch to name a few) are available in many restaurants and are good buys. The restaurant price for any of these wines should be between $6.00 to $12.00 per bottle.

Restaurants usually offer a carafe wine for a modest price. These are almost universally inexpensive California jug wines which are purchased by the gallon (or three or four liters size). The bartender transfers the wine from the gallon jug into a half-liter or full liter wide-mouth carafe. The wines are never exceptional; but they are usually sound, well-made, and drinkable. If the wine list is poor, you will probably not go wrong by ordering the carafe wine.

Some restaurants have their own house wines. These are wines from a relatively obscure vineyard or lesser known shipper. They are bottles which are not generally available in retail stores and which the restauranteur has personally selected for quality and value. They are often very good wines at reasonable prices and usually superior to the restaurant's carafe wine.

A few restaurants do provide competent wine service at reasonable prices. If you are fortunate enough to find one, compliment the personnel and the proprietor and patronize the establishment regularly. Likewise, make known your displeasure with poor wine service and outlandish pricing policies. Refuse a bottle of refrigerated red wine and request one at room temperature. If the wine is served in a dinky three or four ounce glass, request another glass; a large brandy snifter or even a water glass will be an improvement. Tell the wine server not to fill the glasses more than half way. Return chilled wine glasses and request glasses that are not chilled for your red wine. Insist that your red wine be served and opened before you order your dinner; and advise the waiter not to put the cork back into the bottle as is so often ridiculously done.

It is incomprehensible why restaurant owners fail to instruct their personnel on proper care and service of wine, neither of which is difficult or complicated. There is no good reason why a bottle of wine should be opened at the bar and then served to the customer. With a good corkscrew, even the frailest waitress or waiter can remove a cork from a bottle at the table. Certainly with air conditioning in most restaurants a reasonably cool storage location can be found for the wine where it can be stored laying down, rather than standing up in a hot barroom. If the restaurant should happen to have a few good aged wines, certainly the server can be instructed not to hold the bottle by the neck and swing it with each step he takes, obviously stirring up the sediment. If wine buffs will make known their pleasure or displeasure with wine service, eventually restauranteurs will realize that competent wine service and a diversified wine list at reasonable prices are in their own best self-interest and will increase both their wine and food sales.

Wine is the most healthful and hygienic of all beverages.
Louis Pasteur

6

Wine: Beverage, Food, Medicine?

Wine as Beverage

Wine has been a part of man's diet since before the dawn of civilization. Written records, over 4,000 years old, from ancient Egypt establish that wine was made at least 6,000 years ago. Archaeologists have speculated that the beverage of wine was discovered by the cavemen in Mesolithic times about 10,000 years before Christ. Fermented beverages, including wine, were known and used in India and China as well as in Greece and Rome centuries before the birth of Christ. The history of civilization and wine are inextricably intertwined. Throughout the ages, wine has been the beverage used to celebrate the birth of a child, a marriage, and important events of state. Wine had its own gods of Dionysus and Bacchus in ancient Greece and Rome and remains associated with the Hebrew and Christian religions today.

Only in recent times has wine lost the respect and prestige

afforded it by earlier civilizations as a food and beverage. Americans have categorized all alcoholic beverages in the same class with "demon rum" as evidenced by the folly of Prohibition, which failed to distinguish wine, beer, or spirits. Europeans, especially the Latins, do not equate the drinking of wine and the drinking of whiskey and often, subjectively, do not consider wine as an intoxicating beverage. If you ask an Italian whether or not he drinks, he may answer "no" because he drinks only wine. Americans' justifiable concern with alcoholism has created an unjustifiable suspicion and distrust of all alcoholic beverages including wine. Gluttony or the abuse of any beverage or food can be deleterious. Drinking too much iced tea or even water at one sitting can cause illness. There is increasing evidence that wine drinking (unlike the drinking of spirits) reduces the incidence of alcoholism. Most wine-drinking countries such as Italy, Greece, and Southern France have very low rates of alcoholism. Northern France which has a high alcoholism rate is the exception to the rule, probably because of the large amounts of Calvados (apple brandy) consumed. There is a significant relationship between the incidence of alcoholism and the type of alcoholic beverage consumed. In Switzerland, Northern Russia, Finland, Sweden, and Poland which have high rates of alcoholism, the beverage is a form of distilled spirits such as whiskey or vodka. There is some evidence that America's recent romance with wine is having the beneficial effect of reducing our alcoholism rate. In 1974, the Department of Health, Education and Welfare in its Second Report to Congress on Alcohol and Health reported that persons who are mostly wine drinkers are least likely to have alcohol-related problems. Other recent American studies have related the increased consumption of table wine, especially white wine, during the past twenty years to more moderate drinking and a statistical decrease in alcoholism. No one would seriously contend that wine drinking will solve the problem of alcoholism any more than Prohibition solved the problem. The reasons for and causes of alcoholism are far too complex for such simple and superficial solutions. The major reasons for the high incidence of alcoholism in spirit-drinking countries as opposed to wine drinking countries are the social and cultural attitudes toward alcohol. In wine-drinking countries, wine is a part of the daily diet of children and adults; a man does not have to prove his virility by excessive drinking; and intoxication is not socially acceptable. In these countries, wine is drunk almost exclusively with food. In spirit-drinking countries, spirits are drunk between meals not with food. Most groups which look upon alcoholic beverages as a food or an adjunct to the daily diet will have lower incidences of alcoholism than those who look upon it solely as a beverage. Thomas Jefferson recognized this conclusion when he wrote, "No nation is drunken where wine is cheap, and none sober where the dearness of wine substitutes ardent spirits as the common beverage."

Wine as Food

Wine is a food because it provides energy and contains most of the minerals and some of the vitamins which are necessary nutrients for the maintenance of the body. Although wine is not an essential food, it can be useful and beneficial as a dietary supplement. It is an extremely complex beverage of over 300 compounds, including alcohols, aldehydes, acids, esters, polyphenols, carbohydrates, vitamins, and minerals. As a source of energy, the average bottle of dry table wine, white or red, contains about 600 calories or about 90 to 100 calories per single four-ounce serving.

The B-complex vitamins are present in wine in significant and useful amounts. Significant amounts of the daily minimum requirements of the B vitamins of riboflavin (13% to 18%), pyridoxine (52% to 94%), niacin (5% to 14%) and pantothenic acid (2% to 5%) are present in the wine, and all are essential to the normal diet. A riboflavin deficiency can cause ocular problems. Pyridoxine aids metabolism. Niacin is effective against pellagra and pantothenic acid is a growth stimulating vitamin.

Although fresh grapes contain significant amounts of vitamin C, (ascorbic acid), most of this vitamin disappears in the crushing, fermentation, and aging of the wine since vitamin C oxidizes easily. Yet, there are numerous, respected, authoritative wine writers (Alexis Lichine, Harold J. Grossman, Dr. E. A. Maury, and Dr. Gerard Debuigne) who refer to the presence of vitamin C in wine. This is obviously one of the many areas concerning the nutrient value of wines in which further research is warranted.

Wine is also a source of the little known vitamin P. Vitamin P has also been referred to as factor P because it is not truly a vitamin in the technical definition of the word. A vitamin is a food factor that is essential in small quantities to maintain life as well as to enhance growth and reproduction. The absence of a certain vitamin will cause the body to develop a "deficiency disease" which can be reversed by feeding sufficient amounts of the missing vitamin. Vitamin P consists of substances which strengthen the capillaries which are the tiny blood vessels which carry nutrients to the muscles and other tissues. Vitamin P is not a single definite chemical entity as are most other vitamins. The tannins in wine contain these vitamin P properties. The beneficial tonic effects of wine have been attributed to its vitamin P content and certainly wines taste better than black strap molasses or cod liver oil.

Wine contains at least traces of all thirteen minerals necessary to human life. There are appreciable amounts of potassium, magnesium, calcium, phosphorus, and especially iron. Although it has been a common belief that port wine is rich in iron, red table wine contains more iron and is even better for the treatment of iron deficiency anemia than the port.

All wines contain some amount of residual sugar after the fermentation process. The drier the wine, the less the sugar. Dry table red and white wines may contain as little as 0.1% sugar to 2.0%. Sweet white wines such as sauternes may contain up to 4% to 5% residual sugar. Dry sherry will contain only 1% to 2% of sugar, whereas the sweet cream sherries may contain as much as 12% residual sugar.

Wine as Medicine

Physicians throughout civilized history have been prescribing wines for innumerable medical problems. Salvatore P. Lucia, M.D., Professor Emeritus at the University of California School of Medicine, and perhaps the leading American advocate of the medicinal values of wine, has called wine "the oldest medicine" and "the most important medicinal agent in continuous use throughout the history of man." Ancient Egyptian papyri about 1,500 B.C. recommended wines as medicine. There are scores of references to the medicinal qualities of wine in the Old and New Testaments of the Bible, as well as in the Talmud. Hippocrates prescribed wine for various medical problems over 400 years before Christ. The medicinal properties of wine have been continuously recognized by all civilizations from the Greeks and Romans through the Middle Ages to the present time. Although it is true that the practice of medicine until relatively modern times was in the hands of priests, magicians, and medicine-men, many of the cures which they learned through trial and error have been scientifically proven to be valid. Of course, many have also been proven to be invalid.

Cyrus the Great, who founded the Persian Empire 500 years before Christ, served wine mixed with water to his troops effectively to prevent dysentery. Throughout history, wine has been used by the armies of many nations for the same purpose. Science has since proven what the ancient armies learned only from experience that wine is a very effective anti-bacterial agent. Galen, the most distinguished physician of antiquity after Hippocrates, used wine in the second century before Christ to bathe the wounds of the Roman gladiators. The wounds so treated did not become infected because of the anti-bacterial properties of the wine. In 1977, Jack Konowalchuk and Joan I. Speirs, scientists of the Canadian Health and Welfare Agency, found that extracts of wine and fruits killed test-tube cultures of viruses that caused cold sores, stomach upsets, and a type of meningitis. These researchers traced the anti-viral properties to the phenols, particularly the tannin, in the grape skins. During the past thirty years, numerous other researchers have confirmed the antibacterial effect of the phenolic compounds in wine and have concluded that the bactericidal power of wine cannot be explained by its alcoholic content alone.

Russell V. Lee, M.D., of Stanford University School of Medicine, called anxiety "the offspring of fear" and "the oldest of all human ailments." He stated that "the caveman threatened by the saber-toothed tiger had the same anxiety as the Wall Street broker in a bear market." Wine is one of the oldest and safest natural tranquilizers known to man. Man's quest for relief from the tensions and anxieties of the pressures of daily living is evidenced by the sale of one million Miltown tablets in the second year they were on the market. But in France where almost everyone drinks wine, the pharmaceutical companies have difficulty selling their Miltowns or other artificial tranquilizers. A few ounces of port or sherry before retiring would substantially reduce the need for sleeping pills to induce sleep and would be much safer, not to mention more pleasant.

Galen also referred to wine as the "nurse of old age." More and more physicians, hospitals, and nursing homes are using wine in geriatric and convalescent care. In addition to inducing sleep, wine is useful as a sedative for the elderly. Generally, the American medical profession, unlike its European counterpart, has neglected the medical uses of wine in most areas other than geriatric medicine. Many American physicians now recognize that wine helps the elderly avoid depression, induces mental and physical relaxation, stimulates the appetite, aids digestion, and assists in the problems of advancing arteriosclerosis. Because of hypertension, diabetes, or kidney or heart disease, many elderly are required to live on special diets which may be very unpalatable. Wine is useful to supplement such a diet to make it more palatable as well as to provide essential vitamins, calories, and minerals. Doctor Vincent Sarley, Medical Director of the Wrightwood Extended Care Facility of Chicago, in a study conducted at the nursing home found that two ounces of table wine served at the evening meal reduced the "gripe reaction" of the patients. The patients were divided into two groups and were asked questions about the food, their rooms, and the hospital atmosphere. When asked whether the food portions were adequate, 100% of the wine group said yes, but 51% of the non-wine group said no. In response to the question, "Was your bed comfortable?" 100% of the wine group were satisfied, but only 57% of the non-wine group were satisfied. In answer to "Have you had enough nursing care?" 93% of the wine group said yes but only 33% of the non-wine group said yes. Wine is now a definite part of the regimen at Wrightwood when consented to by the patient's physician.

The reference to diabetes in the preceding paragraph may shock many who have been led to believe that alcohol is verboten to all diabetic patients. For hundreds of years prior to the discovery of insulin and even after its discovery, European doctors have used dry table wines in the normal diet of a diabetic, both for the physiological and the psychological well-being of their patients. A number of studies conducted in Europe and the United States in this century have produced evidence that wine does not increase blood sugar levels and may even result in hypoglycemia (lower blood sugar levels). Professors M. A. Amerine and V. L. Singleton of the University of California in their highly respected book, *Wine*, stated that "dry wine can be a source of nonsugar calories as well as dietary variety for diabetics and others on restricted diets." However, since Prohibition, most American doctors, unlike their European brethren, will recommend the avoidance of all alcoholic beverages by their diabetic patients. Therefore, it is recommended that no diabetic should drink wine without first consulting a physician who knows the patient well and who is familiar with the sugar and calorie content of the various types of wine.

The tranquilizing and sedative effects of wine are superior to those of distilled spirits. Research by Giorgio Lolli, M.D., founder of the International Center for Psychodietetics, in experiments comparing the effects of wine and the martini cocktail, demonstrated that muscular tension decreased with the ingestion of a dry red wine but increased with a martini. Although the alcohol in wines and spirits is identical, studies have demonstrated that the alcohol in wine is absorbed much more slowly into the blood stream than the alcohol in spirits. Although the reasons for this are not fully understood, it is believed that the various compounds in wines (which are not present in spirits) such as the phenolic acids, tannins, esters, and nitrogenous substances may be responsible for the difference in the absorption rate. Whatever the reasons, the conclusion is well-documented. When wine is drunk with meals, the rate of alcohol absorption is even slower, and the amount of alcohol in the blood stream even lower. What all this means is simply that the feeling of euphoria from drinking wine is slower than spirits in taking effect but lasts longer. Spirits give you a sudden lift but let you down just as fast.

Doctors have used wine and brandy for centuries to control diseases of the heart and blood vessels because alcohol dilates the peripheral blood vessels and improves the flow of blood. Many doctors have described alcohol as second only to the nitrates in relieving anginal pain. In their book "Alcoholic Beverages in Clinical Medicine," Chauncey D. Leak, Ph.D. and Milton Silverman, Ph.D., stated:

> "There is growing evidence that the regular use of alcohol may act in some way to prevent cardiovascular disease, and especially disease of the coronary arteries. Master and others have presented evidence that alcoholic beverages have a definite and positive deterrent action on the development of atherosclerosis and may protect against coronary thrombosis. After studying the incidence of coronary disease in Europe, Nussbaum concluded that coronary disease is significantly less frequent in countries where wine is part of the everyday diet."

In 1979, Dr. Ronald LaPorte of the University of Pittsburgh delivered a paper before the American Heart Association Annual Conference on Cardiovascular Disease asserting that his study of the drinking and eating habits of twenty industrialized countries supported research by others that moderate wine consumption helps protect against heart disease.

White wines, especially sparkling wines, have long been recognized as effective diuretics. White wine has been found to increase and prolong the level of certain antibiotics (aureomycin and terramycin) in the blood stream if taken together. If substituted for other calorie intake, wine has also been useful in treating obesity because of its tension-relieving, tranquilizing effect. Wine has been used for over 2,000 years as a solvent (menstruum) for pharmaceutical preparations. Many patent medicines using wine as a base were sold in drug stores all during Prohibition. The Renault Winery in New Jersey was able to survive Prohibition only by the sale of "Renault Tonic," a concoction composed of beef peptone (powdered beef), sugar, and wine fortified with alcohol, which produced a 44 proof "legal" tonic. The tonic was sold in the surprisingly forthright flavors of port, sherry, and tokay and was distributed and sold nationally in every major drug store in the United States.

In America any discussions of alcohol are inclined to be extremely emotional and lacking in objectivity. The protagonists and antagonists of the use of alcoholic beverages attack the subject with religiouslike fervor; both usually overstating their positions with unsupported allegations and irrelevancies. It is time that further research be undertaken to determine objectively and scientifically the benefits and detriments of alcoholic beverages, especially wine. Most of all, it is important that all alcoholic beverages are not tarred with the same brush. There has been competent research to demonstrate that spirits, beer, and wine react upon the human body in different ways. American doctors and researchers must put aside their puritanical attitude toward alcohol, including wine, and stop looking only for the bad attributes in alcohol and wine. European scientists must put aside tradition and the economic benefits of wine production and stop looking only for the good attributes of alcohol and wine. Certainly wine is not a panacea for all the ills of man, but neither are aspirin nor penicillin. The historic and scientific evidence to support the claims of the beneficial medicinal qualities of wine is too persuasive to ignore. But research on the therapeutic uses and potential uses of wine is incomplete and sometimes inconclusive. Hopefully, continued and extended research and experimentation will confirm the medicinal attributes of wine learned by our ancestors through trial and error and reveal still unknown therapeutic benefits of our favorite beverage.

Never think of leaving perfume or wines to your heir. Administer these yourself and let him have the money.
                                      Martial (A.D. 40–104)

7

The Wine Cellar

A wine cellar is simply a place to store wine. It may consist of a small wooden rack which you can buy in almost any department store or gift shop to hold half a dozen or a dozen bottles of wine, or, a cardboard liquor or wine carton turned on its side, or, it can be an underground room with storage bins to hold thousands of bottles of wine. A cellar may be a hall closet, a spare bedroom, a liquor cabinet, an area in your basement or any cool, dark nook or cranny in your home or apartment. Which is chosen is a matter of personal preference, availability of space, and finances. However, if you are really bitten by the wine bug, you will undoubtedly end up with an area set aside for at least a hundred or more bottles.

A wine cellar is not an affectation or something you maintain to impress your friends with your sophistication and worldliness. It serves a very necessary and utilitarian purpose. The primary purpose of any wine cellar is to give you a storage place to "lay down" the fine wines of the world which require aging. The term "lay down" means precisely what the words say. It means to place the bottles on their sides in a more or less prone position with the neck of the bottle slightly elevated so that any sediment or deposit will settle toward the bottom of the bottle. There are very few wine stores in America where you can purchase wines which are adequately matured and ready to drink. Thus, it is necessary to "lay down" these wines for a number of months or years. This is especially true of good red wines, most of which require many years in the bottle. As a general rule, most white wines do not require bottle age and will taste best when drunk young, within one to three years of the vintage, except for some of the very fine and expensive ones. Therefore, the red wines in a good wine cellar may outnumber the whites by five to one or even more. Usually the number of bottles of white wine in the cellar are merely a sufficient number to satisfy the day-to-day requirements of the cellar owner, enough to take care of needs of a few months or a year. As the cellar grows, the percentage of red wines will increase and correspondingly the percentage of white wines will decrease. Your individual preference will dictate the ratio of reds to whites in your own cellar.

The ideal cellar conditions are those where the temperature of the storage area is maintained at a constant level of approximately 55° Fahrenheit. It is completely dark, with humidity of about 50%, and completely free of vibration. Most of these conditions can be attained in the average American home or even apartment without too much difficulty. Perhaps the ideal temperature condition is the most difficult to attain. Although with modern air conditioning, even this problem is readily solved. Fortunately, the most important part about the temperature is its constancy. A constant temperature of 65° or even 70° will not seriously harm your wine. However, it may cause it to mature more quickly than the wine kept at 55°. The important thing is to avoid sudden changes in temperature. Gradual temperature changes with the seasons will not seriously affect the wine even though your cellar may be 60° in the winter and 70° in the summer. However, keeping any wine at a temperature much in excess of 70° for any long periods of time will be deleterious. And, of course, variations of temperatures between the fifties and the seventies in a matter of days and occurring repeatedly will in all probability destroy fine wines. The cellar should also have some ventilation but not be drafty.

All table wines should be stored laying down on their sides. This is not an eccentricity. It is an absolute necessity in order to keep the cork of the wine wet so that it does not dry and shrivel up thereby causing a deterioration of the wine by oxidation resulting from too much air getting into the bottle. Prior to the invention of the cork in the early 18th century, it was impossible to have long-lived wines. Wines were kept in the wood casks or in ceramic jugs or crocks and had to be drunk young before they turned to vinegar. The only protection for the wine from the air may have been a film of olive oil on top of the jug or some twisted straw used as a stopper. The invention of the cork made possible the laying down and maturing of wine in the bottle. Even today the experts disagree on the effect the cork has on the wine. The older philosophy was that the cork allowed an infinitesimal amount of air to enter the bottle, which chemically reacted with the wine and caused it to age slowly. More current thinking is that no air at all enters the bottle and that wine will mature and age just as well in an hermetically-sealed bottle as it will in a corked bottle. This is still one of the many mysteries about wine that science has not yet finally resolved. You should be aware that a cork does not have an unlimited life. The life of a cork in a wine bottle is about 25 to 30 years, after which the cork will disintegrate. At the end of this time, the cork should be removed and a new cork inserted. Failure to change a deteriorated cork will result in air getting into the bottle and cause the wine to turn to vinegar as a result of oxidation.

All bottles should be laid down with the labels up for two reasons. It is easier to read the label without unduly shaking or disturbing the wines, and it causes any deposit to settle on the side of the bottle opposite from the label. Thus, if you decant the wine, you can look through the side of the bottle as it is poured and avoid getting the sediment into the decanter.

Another advantage of a wine cellar is that it affords an opportunity of purchasing young wines at a relatively modest cost.

Matured wines are always more expensive than the young ones. Many red wines will be too young to drink when they are purchased and may require two to ten or more years of aging before reaching their peak. If a mature, fine red wine is found in a retail store, it will undoubtedly cost at least two or three times the price of the same wine when it was first bottled and shipped. Obviously, if the wine merchant has stored the wine himself for many years, it has cost him money both in the storage expense and the capital investment, and he must pass on these costs to the consumer. By having your own cellar, you, rather than the merchant, supply the storage space and make the capital investment. The cellar also encourages wine purchases by the case to take advantage of the 10% or more discount that most wine stores offer on sales of case lots. It also provides a readily available stock of wine for personal use as well as making it easy to solve a gift problem on the spur of the moment.

You can establish your own wine cellar in a number of ways. There are innumerable types and styles of wine racks commercially available for anywhere from $10 to literally hundreds of dollars. These racks may hold from six bottles to one hundred or more bottles. They may be made of metal, wood, ceramic, or plastic. Also available in varying sizes are wine vaults with temperature and humidity control, which may cost from about $700 to as much as $4,000. All of these facilities are too expensive and in most cases are unnecessary and superfluous. The most economical and perhaps the most satisfying way of creating a cellar is to build your own wine rack at a cost of probably one-tenth the commercial price. For the medium size (150 bottles) to large cellar (over 500 bottles), I highly recommend diamond-shaped bins. For the small cellar of 20 to 100 bottles, I have devised a vertical type rack which I have found quite adequate and extremely easy to construct. A third common type I shall refer to as a scalloped rack. Appendix F contains drawings and specifications for construction of each of these three types of wine racks.

It does not require a master carpenter to construct any of these racks. The only tool necessary is a hammer if you arrange to have all of the lumber pre-cut. For a very modest charge, your local lumber dealer will probably be happy to cut your lumber in accordance with the specifications in Appendix F.

My personal preference is the diamond-shaped bin which keeps the bottles from rolling around when one is removed and also provides the maximum amount of storage space in the smallest area. You will note that the drawings and specifications for the diamond-shaped bins provide you with bins of 11″ by 13½″ and 11″ by 14½″. The bins are much easier to construct by staggering the shelf sizes. Also, the 11½″ by 13½″ bins will hold a full case of Bordeaux wines but is not large enough to hold a full case of Burgundy wine. The 11″ by 14½″ square will hold a full case of Burgundy-style bottles.

While you are constructing your wine racks, especially if they are to be placed in their own room, closet, or cabinet, build a few shelves parallel to the floor. These upright shelves will serve well for storage of your spirits (whiskey, gin, vodka, brandy) as well as your fortified wines such as sherry, vermouth, or port (other than vintage port). Because of their high alcoholic content, spirits and most fortified wines do not improve with age and need not be laid down. They can be kept for years in an upright position.

In stocking your cellar, you should give consideration to purchasing some half bottles (approximately 12 ounces). Half bottles seem to be waning in popularity and may be difficult to find. But, when available, they offer the opportunity of tasting twice as many wines at almost the same cost. They are also convenient if you are eating alone. Keep in mind, however, that the half bottle will mature more quickly than the full bottle and, therefore, should be drunk sooner.

The difficulty of obtaining half bottles gives rise to the question of what to do with the remaining wine if the full bottle is not finished. Save a couple of small, well-cleaned and rinsed, empty soda bottles (preferably the 12 ounce size) with screw caps. If it is anticipated that only half of the bottle may be used, pour the wine immediately upon opening into the clean soda bottle, right up to the brim, screw on the cap and serve the wine from the wine bottle. Save the wine in the soda bottle for future use. Thus, the wine has had minimal exposure to the air and will keep well for a number of days. However, it is not recommended that you return the unfinished wine in the soda bottle to your cellar for any extended period of time.

Stocking a cellar will depend primarily on two factors, availability of space and availability of cash. A modest fifty-bottle cellar will require a space of only about 4′ by 4′ by 1′ (i.e. a space equal to four cardboard liquor cases stacked two over two) and will cost approximately $150.00 to $250.00 to stock. Of course, the cost can vary greatly with your pocketbook and taste. In chapter 10 you will find a list of recommended wines for the new, unsophisticated wine drinker who would like to try a variety of the wines of the world without having to negotiate a second mortgage on the homestead. It contains representative wines of the major wine-producing countries. This suggested fifty-bottle cellar will afford the neophyte the opportunity of exposing his palate to the wonderfully diversified taste of wine. The fifty suggested bottles will only open the door to the great wines of the world. From there, you are on your own. You will then be in a position to pick and choose and build and expand your wine cellar to suit your personal preference, taste, and pocketbook.

Do not stock up your cellar with wines from only one country. There are too many excellent wines from many countries to limit the exposure of your palate to the monotony of only one country's wines. As you experiment with the tasting of the wines of the world, you will undoubtedly develop a preference for the wines of a certain country or a certain area. But, do not stop experimenting. You will also find that your taste, and often even the style of the wine, will change over a period of time. As you experiment with different wines, you will become more discerning and critical. You may be surprised to find some of the wines you thought were very good during your first few years of tasting, you now consider very mediocre or even poor.

You may conclude, as have many others, that a fine, chateau-bottled, Bordeaux wine has no peer. However, don't ignore the many other great wines of the world which are comparable in quality but different in taste. For example, you may love navel oranges, but this does not mean you will not enjoy a temple orange or even a tangerine. Likewise, even if you could afford it, drinking a fine Bordeaux wine all the time would become as monotonous and boring as eating a prime steak every day of the week. A sound, well-made, inexpensive wine for every day drinking will only heighten your appreciation of a fine wine on that special occasion. The old cliché, "too much of a good thing is bad," is especially appropriate for wine drinking.

The Cellar Book

Every serious wine buff keeps a cellar book which is merely a written record of notes and comments on each of the wines which he has tasted. Everyone should keep a cellar book whether the cellar consists of a small wine rack on your mantle, holding six or eight bottles, or a cardboard liquor carton in the closest with ten or twelve bottles in it, or an underground room with a thousand bottles.

The cellar book is almost as important as the wine library. It provides a permanent record of every wine tasted, when it was tasted, the food accompanying it, and personal comments and appraisal of the wine. You should enter in your notes the special occasion (e.g. holiday, birthday, anniversary, or special dinner party) for drinking a fine wine and the names of any guests who were present. If the guests have any comments about the wine, you may also reflect their appraisal in your notes. The keeping of this written record impresses in your memory the name and type of wine which you have drunk. It helps you remember the good and bad vintages, shippers, importers, quality, and prices, so that you will recall them the next time you are wine shopping. It also acts as a diary to reminisce about special occasions or celebrations and the company you enjoyed when you drank the wine.

Wine publications or gift catalogs often advertise leather bound or (more likely) vinyl covered cellar books costing from $10.00 to $30.00. These are an unnecessary extravagance. A simple, loose leaf, three-ring binder is quite adequate and suits the purpose ideally.

Some wine buffs prefer to sweat the label off the bottle and paste it at the top of each page of their cellar book. If you have the time and the patience, this is a very satisfactory method of keeping a cellar book. The most practical thing to do is simply enter the description of the wine in the book (each wine and each vintage on a separate page) immediately upon the purchase of the wine. Then, after drinking the wine, you can turn to the appropriate page and write your notes as to the quality and taste of the wine.

The following is a suggested format for each page of your cellar book. In the upper righthand corner, index the wine by country, color, region, and sub-region, if any. The following are a few examples:

France – Bordeaux – Red
St. Emilion

or

Italy – Tuscany – Red
Chianti Classico

or

Germany – Mosel – White
Bernkasteler

Along the upper lefthand side of the page list the following headings:

Vineyard – (Insert the name of the vineyard, producer, or shipper.)

Vintage – (The year the grapes were grown. The year will be on the bottle. If the bottle does not state a year, it is a non-vintage wine; in which event it is suggested that you also write the date of purchase on the label of the bottle.)

Date purchased – (When you bought the wine.)

Amount purchased – (Number of bottles or cases you bought.)

Where purchased – (Name and address of wine store.)

Price – (How much you paid per bottle, less discount, plus taxes.)

Importer – (Name and address of the importer or distributor. All foreign wines will have the importer's name and address on the label. All domestic wines will have the name and address of the distributor.)

The following is a graphic depiction of a sample page incorporating these suggestions:

France – Rhone – Red
Hermitage

Vineyard –
Vintage –
Date purchased –
Amount purchased –
Where purchased –
Price –
Importer –

(Date – comments)

(Date – comments)

At first your notes may seem very unsophisticated. You may simply comment that the wine was "good" or "bad"; or that you "liked" or "didn't like" it. But as you progress in knowledge and experience, your notes will become more detailed and comprehensive. You will then comment on the color, aroma, taste, bouquet, and aftertaste. After you drink each wine, note the date in your cellar book, followed by a few short sentences or phrases describing your impressions and appraisal of the wine. There need be nothing especially formal about your cellar book. Appendix G contains photocopies of a few pages from my cellar book demonstrating its informality. They may be helpful in assisting you in organizing your own book and comments.

When you begin to set up your personal cellar book, remember there is no magic in the format. You may wish to use all of the suggested concepts or discard all or parts of them. You may devise your own format which will be completely satisfactory for your purposes. The important thing is that you keep notes on most of the wines you taste for future reference and for guidance in future purchases. As a result of keeping a cellar book, you will be amazed at your recall of the names and vintages of the wines and even when and where you drank them, like the French octogenarian reminiscing about the pleasures of his youth. He recalled an evening in Paris and the beautiful young lady with whom he had dinner and spent the night many decades ago. He recollected that the young lady was lovely and elegant but could not recall her name; however, the wine, a Romanée-Conti, 1929, was magnificent.

An alphabetical arrangement of the pages of your cellar book by countries is recommended. As your notes grow, you may find it necessary to keep separate binders for France, Italy, United States and one for all other countries. Each binder should be alphabetically arranged separately under red and white wines by region and sub-region. Your France binder may be divided into sections for Alsace, Bordeaux, Burgundy, Loire and Rhone, which are in turn sub-divided alphabetically by sub-regions, where appropriate. For example, the Bordeaux wines may be arranged under the sub-headings Graves, Margaux, Medoc, Pauillac, Pomerol, St. Emilion, St. Estephe, and St. Julien. The binder for miscellaneous wines may be alphabetical by countries as follows: Argentina, Australia, Austria, Canada, Chile, Germany, Greece, Hungary, Israel, Portugal, Spain, and Yugoslavia.

Whether you decide to adopt the suggested format or create your own, don't be too fussy or fancy. Don't worry about grammar, punctuation, or the other niceties of good writing. You are making your notes for your own benefit and information, not for posterity. Chances are that very few people will ever read your comments. Even if your impressions about a wine seem silly or frivolous, write them down. If a wine is distasteful to you and makes you think of burning rubber, say so. If a wine is pleasing and makes you think of the unique odor of a brand new automobile, say so. Such comments will indelibly impress the taste or aroma of the wine in your mind. The primary purpose of your cellar book is to help you remember the characteristics of the wines you taste. Any comment which will assist you in accomplishing this purpose is a worthwhile comment.

A cellar book also serves as a running inventory of your wines. This record would be very useful in making an insurance claim for theft or loss by fire or other casualty. It would be helpful in proving what wines were lost and in establishing the value of the wines. Unfortunately, little information is available on insuring wines. A homeowner's policy will usually cover the wines in your home as a part of your household contents. However, if your wines are stored in a warehouse or with your wine merchant or are in transit, the problem is more difficult. Most homeowner's policies provide some coverage (usually 10% of the total personal property coverage) for personal property "away from the premises." Therefore, if your homeowner's policy insures your personal property for $8,000.00, your wines in a warehouse or with a wine merchant would be insured for $800.00, which may or may not be adequate as your wine collection grows. If your personal property, including your wines, is to be moved by a professional mover, you have another problem. The liability of most moving companies is limited by law to a minimum, fixed amount per pound, which amount may be inadequate to protect your expensive wines. Before moving your wine cellar, you should check the amount of the mover's coverage. If it is inadequate, call your broker to secure additional coverage. Also read carefully your insurance certificate to be certain the policy does not contain an exclusion for breakage. As your cellar grows in size and value, you would be well-advised to consult a knowledgeable and competent insurance broker to discuss the problems of insuring your wine both on and off your premises. Follow his advice; the premiums you pay may be money well spent.

8

Wine Clubs and Tastings

Wine clubs offer an unparalleled opportunity for expanding your knowledge of wine. At club meetings you will meet with other wine buffs who share a common interest. All wine club members have an almost insatiable desire to learn all they can about wine. Most members of wine clubs, today, are not wine snobs. So you don't have to be embarrassed about your lack of knowledge when you first join a club. Some members are more knowledgeable than others; but all learn from each other. Wine buffs love to show off their knowledge and will answer, or at least, attempt to answer, any question you may pose to them. They will enthusiastically share with you their knowledge whether it be limited or extensive.

You will learn from other club members where the best wine shops are in your area or even in distant areas where you may go on vacations. You will discuss comparative prices of wines in the various wine shops so that you will know what wines are available and where to get the best buys. Wine club meetings afford you the opportunity to compare your appraisal and evaluation of a wine with other members. Some club members are into growing their own grapes and making their own wine. If you are so inclined, useful information can be exchanged. But, most important, wine clubs make it possible to taste and compare a large number of wines within a few hours at the lowest possible cost.

The financial obligations of wine clubs are minimal. The three best known national organizations, American Wine Society, Les Amis du Vin, and The Vintage Society, charge annual dues of $12.50 to $25.00. These dues include subscriptions to their magazines. The American Wine Society publishes its "American Wine Society Journal," quarterly; Les Amis du Vin publishes "Friends of Wine," bi-monthly; and The Vintage Society publishes "Vintage Magazine," monthly. Many local clubs, unaffiliated with any national organization, charge no dues whatsoever. Each member takes a turn at arranging the meetings and bears the nominal cost of notifying the other members of the meetings. Whether the club is independent or a chapter of a national organization, it is customary for each member to chip in to reimburse the host member for the wine, cheese, and bread served at a meeting. Depending upon the price of the wines tasted, this will usually run about $2.50 to $5.00 a person per meeting.

The primary purpose of a wine club is to study and taste wine, and therefore the organizational structure is usually very simple. One member is selected as the chairman or director to coordinate the club's activities and lend guidance to the host member. Meetings are held at the home of the host member, one who volunteers to arrange and preside at the meeting. The host member selects six or seven wines to be tasted, provides the bread and cheese to clear the palate between wines, provides the indispensable wine glasses, and prepares and provides tasting charts and pencils for making notes.

The meeting program consists of two parts: a very brief business meeting and the tasting. There is no good reason why any business meeting of a wine club should last longer than ten or fifteen minutes. At the business meeting, the host member announces the cost for the tasting and the members decide the date, time, place, and host of the next meeting. There may also be discussions about contemplated trips to local wineries or even tours to wine areas either local or foreign. No one attends a wine club meeting to spend an hour or more discussing organizational problems. You attend the meeting to taste, discuss, and enjoy wine. There are various types of club wine tastings and the formality of the tasting may vary substantially with each club.

Whether you join a large or small club is simply a matter of personal preference. Each has something to offer. The large wine club (thirty-five to one hundred or more members) is often sponsored by a local liquor store which is in a position to secure guest speakers from some of the larger wine producers. Although this type of speaker is promoting his own wine or wines of a particular area or country, nevertheless, he is usually knowledgeable and instructive. The large clubs are less personal than the small, and you may find that you know few people, if any, at your first meeting. Of course, if you continue to attend, you will get to know many of the other members. At a small club (fifteen to thirty-five members) you will probably know a number of the members the very first meeting you attend. After your second or third meeting, you will certainly know everyone. The smaller club provides a better opportunity for informal discussion with fellow club members of each wine as it is tasted. There is no reason why you cannot belong to more than one club if you have the time and inclination.

How do you find or locate clubs in your area? Obviously, the recommendation of a friend or friend of a friend is one way. You can determine whether or not the national clubs have any chapters in your area by writing to American Wine Society, 4218 Rosewold Avenue, Royal Oaks, Michigan 48073; to Les Amis du Vin, 2302 Perkins Place, Silver Spring, Maryland 20910; and to The Vintage Society, 139 East 57th Street, New York, New York 10022. Of course, you can simply get together a half dozen friends and form your own unaffiliated wine tasting group.

Tastings

Wine tastings can run the gamut from a "let's get together and drink some wine" party to a black tie dinner with an engraved wine list and menu. The variations in between are limited only by your imagination. The wine drinking party is simply a cocktail party where you substitute a half dozen different wines for the usual cocktails and hard liquor. The formal dinner wine tasting is exactly that, a formal dinner in a fine restaurant with fine wines to accompany each course of the meal. Of course, you can have your own dinner wine-tasting party, which can be an interesting variation on the usual dinner party preceded by too many taste-destroying cocktails. Simply select a different, appropriate wine for each course of your dinner. (See chapter 2.) The first wine is served as the guests arrive, then one with the hors-d'oeuvres, one for each course of the meal, including one for dessert and one for after dinner. This makes a very pleasant evening even if the guests are not knowledgeable about wine. In fact, the unsophisticated guest is often surprised and pleased by the various taste sensations afforded by the variety of wines served.

Most wine clubs conduct formal tastings, although the degree of formality may vary greatly. The "large formal" tasting is usually at a restaurant or hotel. Tables of eight to ten people are arranged with the number of glasses at each place equal to the number of wines to be tasted. The first wine is delivered to the table by a waitress or wine steward after the guest speaker's introductory comments about the wines to be served. A short period of time is allowed for each person to taste the wine, then the speaker discusses it, and so on through six or seven wines. Often the speaker will entertain questions between the serving of each wine. The value of this type of tasting is dependent almost exclusively on the expertise and tutorial ability of the speaker.

The "small formal" tasting is usually conducted at the home of one of the members who acts as the host and presides over the tasting. If the group is small enough, usually up to ten or twelve people, you may sit around the dining room table. Otherwise, the host member simply provides enough chairs and perhaps a few snack tables so that each member will have a place for his wine glass and his tasting evaluation chart. If the members are not familiar with the wines to be tasted, the host member should be prepared to present a brief introduction to each of the wines as they are tasted. Then the host member asks each member to share his evaluation of each wine before moving on to the next. This format allows for thorough discussion and evaluation of each wine. Individual evaluations are made on the tasting chart and then computed to determine the group average. Each member retains his own evaluation chart for future reference. It is interesting to see the variations or amazingly often the uniformity of evaluation. The small formal tasting format is more conducive to social camaraderie and the free and uninhibited exchange of opinion than is the large formal tasting.

One of the most interesting and challenging of all forms of wine tasting is the "blind" tasting. In a blind tasting, the bottles are wrapped or the wine is decanted into a plain decanter so that no one (except the host) knows the wines to be tasted. This eliminates the unconscious influence of the well-known wine or recognized label. At many blind tastings, the "name" wine or expectedly great wine may be rated as mediocre or occasionally even as the poorest wine at the tasting; and some supposedly inferior and far less expensive wine may receive a consensus rating of first or second.

Tasting evaluation charts have been a source of much discussion and argument throughout the wine world for many years. No one has come up with a truly satisfactory numerical system for evaluating wine and probably never will because wine tasting is such an extremely subjective matter. The University of California at Davis, one of the outstanding enological institutions in the world, has developed a twenty-point system of evaluation which is still in general use, often with variations. Innumerable articles have been written criticizing or modifying the Davis System. Other systems have been suggested and different systems are used throughout the world, based on anywhere from ten to one hundred points. Nevertheless, at least in the United States, the twenty-point evaluation seems still to be the usual norm. Appendix E contains an evaluation chart your wine club may find useful. The particular system used is relatively unimportant so long as all of the tasters are using the same system at the same time. Also in Appendix E you will find a less formal tasting chart in which the system of evaluation has been eliminated. This chart may be used with less sophisticated tasters. It simply informs the tasters of the type of wine being presented and its cost and provides a space for personal notes or comments about the wine.

There are many ways of choosing the wines for a tasting. They may be selected by the country of origin. Thus, a tasting may present French wines from Bordeaux, Burgundy, and the Rhone Valley, both reds and whites, or it may be limited to the reds or white. This type of tasting is especially beneficial for the neophyte wine taster who wants to become familiar with the different wines of a country. The wines may be selected by the area of the country, e.g. the reds or whites of the Rhone Valley of France or the Napa Valley of California. This type of selection is referred to as a "horizontal tasting." Another common selection is a specific type of wine from a specific area. This might consist of all red Burgundy wines from the same commune such as Pommard or several Chianti wines from various Chianti producers. This is referred to as a "vertical tasting." An extremely interesting vertical tasting is a selection of the same wine of a single winery. This might consist of six Cabernet Sauvignon wines from six different vintages of one of the prestigious California wineries, such as Beaulieu or Mondavi or Heitz. This type of tasting will demonstrate, often dramatically, the difference in the quality of the same wines from the same producer from year to year.

Aside from the wine and a corkscrew, the paraphernalia required for a wine tasting is minimal and readily available. All that is necessary is one wine glass for each person, a supply of paper napkins, a pitcher of water, an empty bowl, tasting charts, and pencils. The purpose of the water is to rinse the wine glass after tasting each wine. An ounce of water is poured into the empty glass, swished around, and emptied into the bowl. The paper napkin is used to dry the few drops of water remaining in the glass to avoid diluting the next wine. It is also customary to have bread and cheese available to clear the palate between the tasting of each wine. A word of warning must be offered about palate-clearing snacks at serious tastings. Remember that the stars of the tasting are the wines and not the foods. Don't let the preparation of the snacks become a challenge with each member trying to outdo the other with gourmet snacks. This can become expensive and lead to an unhealthy competition among members. A serious wine tasting is not an appropriate forum for the demonstration of a member's culinary prowess.

There are few rules for wine tastings. One cardinal rule generally recognized is no smoking. This is not part of the current campaign to abolish smoking and ostracize smokers. It is not even to cleanse the taste buds of the smoker. For most confirmed smokers, two or three cigarettes during the usual three-hour tasting will not affect their tasting ability, because they have become programmed to the wine and tobacco smoke combination. The purpose of the rule is to avoid interfering with the olfactory senses of the non-smokers who are not so programmed. A second prohibition which is often unthinkingly or inadvertently violated by club members is the wearing of perfume. The use of any perfume, aftershave lotion, or cologne should be absolutely avoided before attending a tasting. The scent will not only interfere with your own tasting senses but also with those of the other tasters.

Since six to eight different wines are usually tasted in a single session, the amount of each wine served should be restricted to approximately two ounces per person. A bottle of wine contains about twenty-four to twenty-five ounces, and simple arithmetic demonstrates that each taster will have had at least one-half bottle in the course of a tasting. If the host member is overly generous with the portions of each wine served, he may find he will have a number of unexpected overnight guests. A serving of two ounces of wine per person also makes it possible for the host to estimate the number of bottles of each wine required for the tasting. A good rule of thumb is one bottle of each wine for every twelve people. Thus, twenty-four tasters would require two bottles of each wine. A problem arises with fourteen to twenty tasters. In this case, there will be too many people for one bottle of each wine and each serving will be "stingy." And, there will be too few people for two bottles of wine, and either the wine will be wasted (which would be a terrible shame) or, more likely, some members may leave the tasting "feeling no pain." This problem can be solved only by requiring club members to make reservations for each tasting and limiting the number to multiples of twelve.

All types of wine tastings are and should be fun. Some are more instructive and informative than others, but they are seldom dull. Conversation may lag during the tasting of the first couple of wines if those present are strangers; however, both conversation and the volume of conversation will surprisingly increase with each wine tasted. There is nothing like a glass or two of wine to relax inhibitions and stimulate discussion. By the fourth or fifth wine, everyone will be talking to everyone else, and the tasting will be a great success.

How to Taste Wine

There is a difference between drinking wine and tasting wine. The wine drinker gulps the wine as a thirst-quenching beverage and pays little attention to its various good or bad qualities. The wine taster sips the wine and analyzes and appreciates the qualities which make it good or bad. The wine drinker knows only that, subjectively, the wine tastes good or bad to him. The wine taster knows why the wine tastes good or bad and recognizes the degrees of quality. Although wine tasting can never be absolutely objective, the wine taster will be far more objective than the wine drinker because of an ability to understand and analyze the components of taste. The development of this ability also leads to a far greater appreciation and enjoyment of wine.

You must know how to taste wine before you can dissect and analyze its tasting components. The first thing you do is look at the wine, then swirl it around in the glass, smell it, take a generous mouthful, swish it around in the mouth to touch all parts of the tongue and teeth, then swallow. As you swallow, open your lips slightly and suck in air with the wine. By this process you are able to assess the basic components of the wine's appearance, nose, taste, and aftertaste. This is the basic tasting process used even by professional tasters with one major exception. The professional taster does not actually swallow the wine but spits it out into a container provided for this purpose. The wine is spit out for the very practical reason of avoiding intoxication since the professional taster will often taste thirty or more wines at a single session.

Wine tasting involves the senses of sight, smell, and taste and to a lesser degree the sense of touch. Most people use these senses almost unconsciously and fail to utilize them to anything even approaching their full potential. Most are inherently lazy, and if something tastes good, don't bother to analyze it any further to determine why. They fail to realize that these senses can be developed and fine tuned to a very high level of awareness. Virtually everyone has the ability to develop them and needs only to make a conscious effort to cultivate them. All it takes is the concentration to think about them as they are used and to detect the different nuances of sight, smell, and taste. However, in order to appreciate these nuances it is necessary to know what to look for.

First, you look at the appearance of the wine. This must be done in a well-lighted room, never in a dingy or dimly lit room where it would be impossible to observe the true color and clarity of the wine. A surprising amount of information may be gained solely from the wine's appearance. Observe the clarity of the wine. Great wines will have a brilliant, sparkling bright appearance not unlike the brilliance and liveliness of a blue white diamond or fine cut ruby. A clear wine lacking in this sparkling brilliance will probably be a good wine but not a great wine. Most commercial wines are well-made and will be perfectly clear and pass the clarity test without difficulty. A dull, hazy, or cloudy wine is usually a poor and often a bad wine. The exception to this rule is the very good wine which normally throws a sediment but has been shaken prior to service, thereby mixing the sediment throughout the wine giving it a cloudy or muddy appearance. Any wine which has thrown a sediment should be decanted (as described in chapter 3) in order to avoid this cloudiness.

Next, you observe the color of the wine. It is red, yellow, rosé, or almost colorless. A white wine although usually a very pale yellow or almost colorless may be tinged with a little green or gold. If you detect a tinge of brown, the wine is probably maderized and over-the-hill, having lost its youthful freshness. The browner the white wine, the older it will be. A purple red wine is usually very young and may or may not be ready to drink. A purple tinge in a Beaujolais or Bardolino is not objectionable because these are wines to be drunk young. However, a good Bordeaux, Burgundy, or Chianti Classico should be aged and lose its purple hue before it is ready to drink. A mature red wine will brown around the edges where the top of the wine meets the glass. This is not objectionable but is indicative of the age of the wine. The browner the wine, the older it is. A really brown color denotes a wine which is badly oxidized and probably not drinkable.

Other things to look for are the presence of bubbles and the viscosity of the wine. If the wine appears to be light and watery, it will likely taste the same way. If it appears to be heavy and thick, it will usually be a rich, full-bodied wine. After you swirl the wine in the glass, you may notice rivulets of wine above the wine level. These are referred to as the legs of the wine. In the past the legs were thought to be caused by the high glycerin content of the wine. The more modern and probably correct theory is that the legs are caused by evaporation of the alcohol in the wine.

After observing appearance, smell the wine. The sense of smell is the most important component of wine tasting. Many confuse the senses of smell and taste which are quite distinct, although indispensable complements of each other. The mouth and tongue can taste only salt, sweet, sour, and bitter. All other "tastes" are in reality odors, which are virtually infinite. If you are blindfolded and hold your nose, you would have difficulty distinguishing between a bite of an apple and a bite of an onion, because the difference is in the odor not in the taste. It is next to impossible to taste wine if you have a bad cold because the nasal passages are obstructed and you are unable to appreciate the smells emitted by the wine.

The smell or nose of the wine, as it is often called, is divided

into aroma and bouquet. Although they are often used synony-
mously, aroma and bouquet are two separate components. Aroma
is that odor which is unique to the variety of the grape from
which the wine is produced. The classic wine grapes such as
Cabernet Sauvignon, Riesling, Pinot Noir, and Nebbiolo produce a wine with a characteristic and uniquely discernable
smell. Repeated tastings of the varietal wines will firmly fix the
different grape aromas in your mind and make them readily
recognizable. The bouquet is the smell of the volatile esters and
aldehydes emanating from the wine and develops from the
chemical changes that result from the making and aging of wine.
The esters and aldehydes are those perfume-like vapors given
off by the wine as it oxidizes upon exposure to the air. A fine
wine with great finesse will have an intense and lingering bouquet but yet be light and delicate. It will also have a very complex bouquet of numerous overtones of different pleasing and
harmonious smells of various fruits and flowers. The bouquet of
a good wine will not be sharp or harsh, indicating that the alcoholic content is out of balance, but will be a mellow blending of
the volatile acids and alcohol and the aroma.

Occasionally, especially in a white wine, you will detect the
odor of sulphur which is often used to kill the bacteria in wine
barrels and in the wine itself. Prudent use of sulphur will not
affect the quality of the wine and any vestiges remaining in the
bouquet will usually dissipate after being open to the air for a
few minutes. Another common smell of wine is referred to as
the smell of wood or oak. A woody or oaky smell is not necessarily undesirable unless it is overpowering. The smell of oak or
wood in a wine is recognizable because it is very similar to the
smell of vanilla extract. Proper aging in wood will add to the
complexity and interest of the wine. Too much wood age will
produce a wine with an excessive wood or oak nose which over-
powers the other smells of the wine. Most wines will also have
an almost undetectable smell of acetic acid which is vinegar. If
the vinegar smell is outstanding or predominant, the wine is
undoubtedly bad and has, in fact, turned to vinegar.

The four tastes of salt, sweet, sour, and bitter are detected by
the tongue. Each portion of the tongue performs a different job.

Salt, which is unimportant in wine tasting, is transmitted to the brain from the sides of the tongue. Sweet is detected at the tip of the tongue; sour (acid), at the upper edges; and bitter, at the back. The taste of sour and bitter can occasionally be confusing. By knowing where to detect these tastes on the tongue, you will be less likely to confuse the two.

The taste of sweetness is basic and self-explanatory. Everyone seems to be born with a sweet tooth as evidenced by the fact that all children like candy, cake, and ice cream. The tastes of sour and bitter seem to be acquired tastes which develop with maturity. Because of this, many new wine drinkers start with the sweeter wines and graduate to the drier ones.

Although there is an element of sourness in all wines, a wine which is truly sour is a bad wine. The sourness in wine is caused by acidity, and wine tasters use the term acid or acidity rather than sour or sourness unless the wine is in fact bad and turning or turned to vinegar. A wine with inadequate acid will be dull, flat, and lifeless, often referred to as flabby. It is not uncommon for the new wine taster to confuse acid and alcohol. Alcohol is detected primarily by sharpness in the nose and acid by the sourness on the tongue.

Bitterness is more often found in red wines than in white wines. Again, since bitterness is an acquired taste, most new wine drinkers favor whites over reds. Bitterness in wines is not an undesirable trait if it is not excessive. The bitterness is caused by the tannins which are extracted from the skins, seeds, and stems of the grapes in the fermentation process. It will be detected in the aftertaste in the back of the mouth and tongue after the wine has been swallowed. White wines have little or no tannin because they are fermented from the juice of the grape from which the seeds, skins, and stems have been separated. Because of this usual method of fermenting white wines, they can be made from black, red, or white grapes. If you have any doubt about this, peel a black or red grape and you will see that the meat is the color of white wine. Most great French champagnes, which are, of course, white, are produced from the Pinot Noir grape which is black. The color of red wine is extracted from the grape skins in the fermentation process. Closely related to bitterness is astringency, which is a feeling rather than a taste. It is that puckery feeling also caused by the tannins that makes the mouth pucker at the sides of the cheeks like the sensation of eating a persimmon. It draws the mouth and can also be felt on the front teeth.

The sense of touch comes into play in wine tasting only in assessing the characteristic of body of the wine. The body is the weight, the lightness or heaviness, of the wine in the mouth. A full bodied wine has a heavy feeling, and is one you can almost chew. A light-bodied wine is light in the mouth and thin and watery. Body relates to the viscosity of the wine which is increased by higher alcohol or sugar content of the wine.

In a great wine, all of the tasting components blend together and balance in a symphony of pleasing sensations. The nose is complex and well-balanced with none of its volatile alcohols or acids overpowering the others. The taste of sweet, sour, and bitter are in harmony and blend together like the music of a great orchestra. No single tasting component stands out among all the others. The wine will have a long lingering aftertaste remaining in the mouth and nasal passages after the wine is swallowed.

Wine tasting requires no special talents. Nothing more is required than normal senses of sight, smell, and taste and a conscious effort to develop these senses. There is no substitute for experience which is the major difference between the amateur and the professional wine taster. An expert wine taster will also have an excellent memory. He can often remember and recapture the taste of a wine he drank ten or twenty years earlier. However, he does not rely on memory alone. He also makes notes of every wine he tastes. (See chapter 7.) Perhaps the most difficult aspect of wine tasting is communicating to others your impressions and assessment of a wine. Every business, profession, and discipline has its own language. A doctor, lawyer, engineer, or tradesman must learn the vocabulary of his vocation. Wine tasting is no different. The wine buff must learn the lingo of his hobby in order to communicate intelligently and effectively with other wine buffs. (See Glossary.) A word of caution, however. Don't fall into the trap of meaningless jargon like the famous cartoon character of James Thurber who gave the following description of a wine: "It's a naive domestic burgundy without any breeding, but I think you'll be amused by its presumption."

I often wonder what the vitners buy.
One half so precious as the stuff they sell.
Omar Khayyam

9

Wineries and Wine People

Wine is grown in every continent in the world. It is now made commercially in over half the states of the United States, in most of the countries of Europe, in South America, in Australia, and even in some small amounts in the Far East. Wineries may vary in size from a few acres to thousands of acres. The best known extremes are the internationally famous wineries of Romanée Conti in Burgundy, France, and E. & J. Gallo in California. Romanée Conti produces about fourteen hundred gallons of wine each year, and Gallo produces over sixty million gallons per year. The winery may be a small family operation, or a subsidiary of a large conglomerate corporation, or a cooperative with a membership of fifteen or over fifteen hundred growers. During the past ten years there has been a trend of takeovers of many of the large and famous wineries throughout the world by the corporate conglomerate. For example, Heublein now controls Beaulieu Vineyards and Inglenook in the Napa Valley of

California as well as the Italian Swiss Colony and Petri Wineries in California. Even the soft drink giants of Coca Cola and Pepsi Cola have gotten into the act, respectively, with the Mogen David Winery and the Hudson Valley Wine Company in New York. Seagrams owns numerous wineries throughout the world, including the famous Italian wineries of Bersano in Piedmont and Brolio in Tuscany, as well as Paul Masson in California.

Fortunately, it appears, at the present time, that the conglomerate management has not adversely affected the products of most of the wineries which were purchased. However, it is still a little too soon to determine what the ultimate long-term effect of the conglomerate takeovers will be.

People and Philosophy

Most wine people, regardless of the size of the winery, are the greatest. To paraphrase Will Rogers, "I have never met a wine man I didn't like." They are interesting, gregarious extroverts who love people, good food, and good wine. They literally glow with pride if you express your satisfaction with one of their wines. If you dislike one of their wines, they will continue to open bottles of their other wines until they find one that pleases you. They seem never to tire of discussing their wines and are sincerely interested in your opinion. You don't have to pull any punches. They are not offended by an honest, intelligent criticism of their wines. All are continually experimenting with new processes and new equipment to improve their products. Each winemaker has his own theories on growing and producing the best wines possible. He will eagerly discuss the merit of aging in wood or stainless steel or fiberglass, and whether the wine should be aged for six months or six years before bottling.

The current philosophy of many winemakers throughout the world is to produce wines which are drinkable as soon as they are bottled or shortly thereafter. These modern enologists are attempting to meet demands of today's consumer who is too impatient to lay down his wines for ten years before drinking them. They are filtering, fining, and clarifying their wines to eliminate all traces of sediment. Many are eliminating the use of wood casks completely, even for their red wines. One respected enologist from Northern Italy explained this philosophy by analogizing wine to certain foods. He pointed out that one hundred years ago, it was necessary to smoke ham to preserve it because of the lack of refrigeration and modern methods of preservation. Thus people became used to the smoky taste even though it may taste terrible. Likewise, wine was aged in wooden barrels because wood was the only satisfactory material at the time. Stainless steel and fiberglass were unknown. The consumer became accustomed to the taste of wood even though it detracts from or even destroys the true fruit taste of the wine. It is his conclusion that the fermentation and aging of wine in modern materials imparts no foreign flavor to the wine and produces a fruitier, truer to the grape, more varied flavor than wood aging. This modern philosophy is especially evident in many of the wines of California, Burgundy, and some areas of Italy.

The traditionalists believe that the excessive filtering and clarifying of the wines and the abandoning of aging in wood, not only eliminates sediment, but also eliminates quality. They believe that the modern technology produces mediocre wines lacking in the character, complexity, and finesse of wines made in the traditional wood barrels. Their position is that the modern enologists are filtering all the life out of the wine and merely producing fermented grape juice, which may be very drinkable, but is dull, flat, and uninteresting. They are concerned that the continued acceptance of the modern methods will ultimately eliminate the fine vintage wines (especially reds) which are ready to drink only after eight or ten years of age and which may live for many decades after bottling.

Many of the European wineries have been in the same family for centuries. The owners take great pride in their history and heritage. The chateau, villa, or castle in which they live is often hundreds of years old, historically significant, and magnificently appointed with works of art and antiques. They may show you their "ancient" wine labels, about which they will speak with almost religious fervor. Their old wine cellars are often caves in the ground carved out of the subterranean rock. The heads of the barrels may be beautifully hand carved with decorative winery scenes. Some of the older casks may even be called by name. In the Rallo Winery in Marsala, Sicily, there are two huge oak barrels over one hundred years old which are named Trento and Trieste, which are the names of the first two towns liberated by the Allies in World War I. There is an aura of immortality about many of the family-owned wineries. The owners antici-pate that their children, as well as their children's children, will carry on the business. It is a way of life.

Winery Visits

Wineries are often in or near historic or resort areas. They may be at the seashore, in the plains, or in the mountains. They offer the vacationer, whether in America or overseas, the oppor-tunity to combine sightseeing with winery visits. Most wineries have attractive and comfortable tasting rooms where the visitor can taste their wines without charge. Some have restaurants on the premises where their wines can be enjoyed with a leisurely meal; or there may be a picnic area where you can bring your own picnic lunch and spend the afternoon. Many have museums where fascinating collections of wine glasses, wine bottles, cork-screws, casks, presses, or other winemaking equipment and paraphernalia are displayed. Some of the European wineries have collections of ancient artifacts over 2,000 years old, which were dug out of their own vineyards. There is often a gift shop where knickknacks, wine books, and wine paraphernalia may be purchased.

A wine club or personal visit can be arranged at most wineries by a simple telephone call or preferably a letter. A letter explain-ing your particular interest in wine with a request to visit the winery between certain dates is the most effective way of ar-ranging an appointment. The letter will usually bring a response suggesting that you telephone the winery upon your arrival in the area to fix a firm date and time for the visit. Some wineries have periodic, daily, guided tours, and no appointment is neces-sary. Abroad, the foreign trade commissions and tourist offices, both their offices in the United States and their overseas offices, are extremely helpful and cooperative in assisting with arrangements for winery visits.

Whether the winery produces five thousand or five million gallons of wine per year, a visit is an interesting, informative, and fascinating experience. It will usually start at the stemmer-crusher machines, which remove the stems from the grapes and crush them. The resulting mass is called the must. The stemmer-crusher machine may be outside the winery building so that the trucks, coming in from the vineyards, can dump the grapes into the machine without entering the building. The must proceeds from the stemmer-crusher machines into the pressing machines in the building where it is pressed to squeeze the juice from it. Sulpher dioxide is usually added to the must after it is pressed in order to destroy undesirable micro-organisms and inhibit the enzymes which cause wine to turn brown. From the pressing machines the must is piped to the fermenting tanks. For red wine, both the skin and the juice go into the fermenting tanks. For white wine, only the juice of the grape, without the skins, is placed in the fermenting tanks. The pigmentation and color of wine come primarily from the skins of the grapes. This is the reason that white wine may be made from black or red grapes as well as white grapes.

Fermentation is the process which converts the sugar of the grape into alcohol. Thus the higher the sugar content of the grape, the higher the alcoholic content of the wine. Grape sugar is usually measured in Brix, which is sometimes referred to as "degrees balling." Brix is the percentage of natural grape sugar in the grape juice. By measuring the Brix of the grapes or the must, the winemaker can estimate the alcoholic content of the wine to be produced from the grape juice. If the juice measures 20 Brix, it can be anticipated that it will produce a wine of approximately 11% alcohol; or to state it another way, the alcohol by volume will be slightly more than one half the Brix. If the sugar content of the grape is too low, it may be necessary to add sugar (Chaptalisation) to the must. Chaptalisation is common in Germany and France but is not permitted in California or Italy.

After fermentation which may take from one to six weeks, depending upon the type of wine, the temperature at which the wine is fermenting, and the philosophy and style of the wine-maker, the wine is placed into aging containers. These containers may be wood, concrete, stainless steel, or fiberglass. Here it will remain for months or years, again depending upon the type of wine to be produced and the style of the enologist. It may for the first number of months remain in stainless steel or fiberglass for clarification (fining) and then be transferred to wood casks or other tanks for further aging. When you see the must, which even for white wine looks dirty and muddy, you will wonder how this ugly mess ever becomes the clear white or pale yellow liquid of wine. But over the centuries the winemakers have learned to remove the dirt and particles suspended in the wine to produce the expected brilliant, sparkling colors of white and red wines. There are numerous methods used for filtering and clarifying wine. The methods will depend upon the sophistication, modernization, and tradition of the winery. One of the oldest fining elements, which is still used in some small wineries, is egg whites. But today, mechanical filters, not unlike the filters in your air conditioner or heater, are in common use along with inert filtering chemicals which precipitate the colloidal particles in the wine. Many of the very modern plants use refigeration and freezing to precipitate the sediment and particles.

After the wine is clarified, it is placed into the aging containers which may be wooden barrels or tanks holding only a couple thousand gallons each or large stainless steel or fiberglass tanks each holding ten thousand gallons or more. Many of the large commercial wineries will have aging or storage tanks thirty to forty feet high containing one hundred thousand gallons of wine.

If you are fortunate, you may be afforded the opportunity to taste the wine from the barrel or the tank. Don't expect too much. You must recognize that these wines are not finished nor ready to drink. But, with a little experience, much can be learned about the unfinished wine. The basic attributes of the wine are present at this early stage, and you can make an educated guess and prognosis about the future of the wine and what to anticipate about its quality and longevity.

The matured and finished wine is then bottled and labeled. The small wineries may still bottle and label the wine manually.

But most of the larger, modern wineries have very sophisticated and efficient bottling machinery which can fill from twenty-five hundred to eight thousand bottles per hour, including the insertion of the cork, the placing of the capsule over the cork, and the application of the label. One of the most impressive attributes of all wineries is cleanliness. Whether the winery is tiny of enormous, you will find that you can virtually eat off the floor. This is necessary not only to protect the consumer, but also to protect the investment of the producer. During the fermentation and aging processes, wine can be very unstable and subject to a multitude of bacterial invasions. The winery must be spotless to avoid the introduction of any foreign matter or bacteria which can literally destroy thousands of dollars of wine.

After your tour of the winery, you may be invited to visit the vineyards. This is an equally fascinating experience. A well-maintained vineyard is indeed a beautiful sight, especially when the vines are laden with ripe grapes. Here you will learn something about the various methods of growing and pruning the vines, which will vary immensely depending upon the climate and the nature and contour of the land and the subsoil. The quality of any wine depends upon the quality of the grapes used. The most knowledgeable and sophisticated enologist cannot produce a good wine from poor grapes. Most of the world's best wines are made by producers who grow their own grapes rather than purchasing grapes from others. The control of the growing methods is just as important as the control of the vinification processes. Your guide will show you the various varieties of grapes grown in the vineyard and explain why the particular varieties are grown rather than others. Wineries are continually experimenting with various grape varieties to improve their end product. You will learn how the vagaries of weather affect the grapes and the quality of the wine from year to year. Hail is a mortal enemy of the vineyard. A hail storm can destroy a vineyard and cause it to be unproductive for one or two subsequent years. A serious storm may destroy the vineyard and necessitate a complete replanting. A newly planted vineyard will not produce grapes of sufficient quality or quantity for at least three years, and usually four to five years after planting. Although a

grapevine may live fifty to a hundred years, it has a commercially productive life of twenty to twenty-five years, after which
time the per acre production substantially decreases. Although
the quality of the grapes from a forty-year-old vine is usually
very high, the quantity produced usually makes it uneconomical
to continue cultivation.

Winery and vineyards visits are an integral part of the education of every wine buff and are necessary to a full and complete
understanding and appreciation of wine. They also offer a most
pleasurable way of acquiring an abundance of wine knowledge
with a minimum of effort. But, most of all, the congeniality and
generosity of wine people is overwhelming. Perhaps, H. W.
Yoxall, a prominent British wine journalist, summarized it best
when he said:

> "Looking back, after a lengthy and diverse experience of business,
> I can say with assurance that I have never met in any other trade
> such a pleasant body of men as those who are in wine."

Wine is a constant proof that God loves us and loves to see us happy.

Benjamin Franklin

10

Digest of Wines of the World

Now that you know the basics of stocking a cellar, serving and tasting wine, you must decide what wines you will purchase to expose your palate to the almost infinite variety of wine styles and tastes. With the ever-escalating prices of wine, it has become increasingly difficult for the new wine buff to experiment and learn about the wines of the world at affordable prices. This digest will offer the neophyte the opportunity to make such experimentation without spending a small fortune in the learning process. It is not intended, nor does it presume to be a substitute for, the many wine textbooks which are readily available. It supplies basic information about the major wine countries. The serious student will refer to the books listed in Appendix D for in-depth study.

The wines designated with an asterisk are the fifty wines with which the wine buff may start his first wine cellar. The suggested wines are not necessarily the best, but are good examples of the type or style of a particular wine at economical prices. Most of the recommended wines can be purchased for under $5.00 a bottle, many at less than $3.50. All fifty wines can be purchased for about $200.00. The wines without the asterisk will retail for about $5.00–$15.00 a bottle. None of the wines listed should cost more than $15.00 per bottle, and most should retail for under $10.00 per bottle.

The best wine buys will be made from a reputable wine dealer. The liquor store which sells mostly spirits and has a small wine selection should generally be avoided for the purchase of quality wines. The store that specializes in wine will offer better buys and better quality and selection. It will have a relatively fast turnover of inventory, and it is less likely that its wines will have been improperly stored, badly maderized, or over-the-hill. The wine specialist will also furnish honest advice about the wines he is selling. He will have available vintage charts to assist in evaluating the relative merit of the wines of each harvest year. Most vintage charts are on a scale of 1 to 10 with 10 being the highest rating possible. The following is a vintage chart which is printed on the back of the membership card of the American Wine Society.

	Vintage →	70	71	72	73	74	75	76	77	78	79	Past Greats (best)
RED	Bordeaux	9b	8c	3c	6c	6b	9a	8a	4a	7a	7a	66b, 64c, 61c, 59d
	Burgundy	7d	9c	7c	5c	5c	3c	10a	6a	7a	7a	69c, 66c, 64d, 61c
	Rhone	9b	7c	6c	5c	5b	4b	9a	5a	8a	7a	69c, 67c, 64c, 61c
	Italy	8c	10b	3d	6c	8b	7b	6b	6b	8a	9a	67c, 64c, 61d
	CA Cabernet	9c	6c	4c	7c	10b	6b	7a	6a	7a	7a	68d, 64d
WHITE	Bordeaux	8b	8c	2d	6c	4c	9a	8a	4b	7a	8a	67c, 62c, 61c, 59c
	Burgundy	8c	10c	5c	8c	7c	8b	9b	6b	7a	8a	69c, 66c, 64d, 62d
	Loire	8c	9c	4d	7c	6c	8c	10b	4c	7a	8a	69c, 67c, 61c, 59d
	Germany/Alsace	7c	10c	4d	7c	5d	9b	10b	6b	6a	7a	69c, 67c, 64d, 59d
	CA Chardonnay	8d	8d	6d	7d	8c	9c	8b	7a	8a	7a	(Too Old)
	Champagne	7c	9c	—	8c	7b	9a	10a				69c, 66d, 64d, 61d
	Port	9a	—	—	—	—	7a	—	10a	8a		66c, 63b, 60c, 55c

10 = Best   a young   b improving   c ready   d declining

Figure 9

It has been said many times that one should not be a slave to a vintage chart and that they are merely guides, not mandates. Weather is one of the most important factors affecting any vintage. Within a given country or even a given area, the weather can vary substantially. Vineyards only a few miles apart may have had varying amounts of rain resulting in higher or lower sugar content of the grapes. The skill of the winery (and sometimes luck) in harvesting the grapes at just the right time will affect the wine to be produced. The talent of the winemaker is always an important factor in the quality of the wine. Because of all of these variables, some wineries may produce excellent wine in "off years" and others poor wines in good years. However, vintage charts are useful in the absence of any other guidelines. For example, if you have not tasted a particular wine, or if your wine merchant cannot make a recommendation and you have nothing else to assist you in your choice, you should certainly purchase a wine with a higher vintage chart rating. This does not guarantee that the higher rated wine will be better than the lower, but it increases your odds of getting the better wine.

The date on the bottle of wine is the "vintage" and is usually the date the grapes were harvested. Thus, if a bottle of wine carries the date "1975," this means the grapes were picked in 1975. The wine may have been bottled any time after that. A vintage date is merely an indication of the age of the wine and not the quality of the wine. All the producer is saying is that the grapes or most of them from which the wine was made were harvested in 1975. A non-vintage wine is one without any vintage date on the label, and therefore, may be a blend of wine from various years. This blending produces a consistency in the wine which is impossible to achieve without such blending. However, it usually also produces only mediocre wine and not great wine. Even wines with a vintage date may have small amounts or percentages of wine from other years blended into the wine of the vintage year. The extent to which such blending is permissible will vary with the laws of the country in which the wine is produced.

The term vintage year does have a special meaning or connotation when used on a bottle of champagne (French) or port (Portugese). Most champagnes are not vintage dated but are wines blended from different years and should be consumed at a relatively young age. However, in a particularly good year, the champagne producer will declare a vintage and produce and bottle a wine carrying a vintage date. This will be a superior champagne and invariably will be more expensive and usually longer-lived than ordinary bottlings of champagne. A similar process is used with port wines. During an extremely good year, the port producer will declare a vintage and produce a wine only from the grapes from that vintage, unblended with wine from other vintages.

Although the higher-priced wines are usually the better wines, this is not necessarily true. Certain wines, such as a Pouilly Fuissé and Chateauneuf-Du-Pape, have names that have caught on with the American consumer and sell at prices far in excess of their intrinsic value because of the laws of supply and demand. Unfortunately, for the consumer, the prices of most of the fine French wines are becoming prohibitive, and the wine buff is more and more turning to wines from other countries and domestic wines for good wines at reasonable prices. Many of the wines from Italy, Spain, Portugal, Austria, Chile, Australia, Yugoslavia, Hungary, and our own American wines are of excellent quality at modest cost.

Wine value cannot be appraised by quality alone at the exclusion of price. A $25.00 bottle of fine French or German wine will probably be superior to a $5.00 bottle of California or Italian wine; but it will not be five times as good. Often the quality difference may be so subtle that the new wine buff, because of lack of tasting experience, may be unable to distinguish it. By experimenting first with tasting the affordable, lower-priced wines, the beginner will appreciate the nuances of flavor and finesse of the occasional, fine, expensive wine.

France

It is generally conceded that the French wines set the standard by which all great wines are judged. So great has been the influence of French wine upon other wine producing countries, that even certain bottle styles are referred to internationally as

Bordeaux type (Figure 10) and Burgundy type (Figure 11). Germany, with some justification, may challenge the French superiority in the production of white wine, and in recent years, the great wines of California are successfully competing with the French wines. One should not make the mistake of selecting a wine merely because it is French. France does not have a monopoly on the great wines of the world. Every serious wine-producing country produces at least some superb wines. There are many fine French wines, but there are also many inferior ones, just as there are in every other country.

All good French wines are produced in delimited areas designed by the French laws of the Appellation d'Origine Contrôlée (AOC). The beginning wine buff should avoid any French wine which does not have the words "Appellation Contrôlée" on the label. These words guarantee that the wine is produced only from certain specific grapes grown only in a defined geographic area. The AOC laws also control the quantity of grapes produced per acre of vineyard, the methods of pruning the vines, and the minimum alcoholic content of the wine. These laws establish only minimum standards, and the great wineries of France produce wines which far exceed the minimums. It must be emphasized that the words "Appellation Contrôlée" do not guarantee the quality of the wine, but only its place of origin and that it has met with the minimum standards. As a general rule, the narrower and more specific the AOC designation, the better the wine will be. For example, the Bordeaux region of France is divided into the five major sub-areas of Medoc, Graves, Pomerol, St. Emilion, and Sauternes. The Medoc area in turn is sub-divided into communes of which Pauillac, St. Julien, St. Estephe, and Margaux are the major ones. Within each commune are the Chateaux, the individual vineyards. Thus, a Chateaux-bottled wine from a specific vineyard in the Pauillac commune is considered superior to a commune wine which may be a blend of wines from a number of different vineyards in the commune, although the label on both wines will read "Appellation Pauillac Contrôlée." The commune wine should be superior to a Medoc wine which may be a blend of wines from a number of different communes. In turn, a Medoc wine is considered

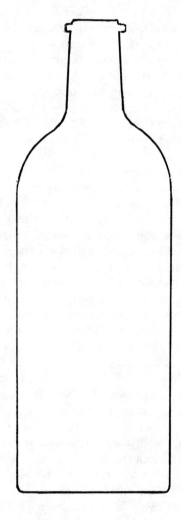

Figure 10

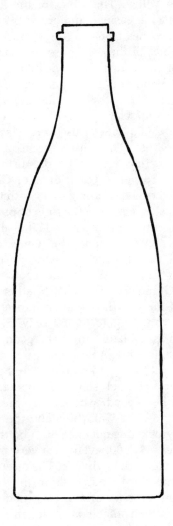

Figure 11

superior to a Bordeaux wine which may be a blend of wines from anywhere in the entire Bordeaux region.

The three major wine areas of France are Bordeaux, Burgundy, and Rhone Valley. The wines of the Loire Valley and Alsace are becoming increasingly important because of the escalating prices of the wines from the three major areas. Perhaps the greatest red wines of the world are the clarets produced in the Medoc area of Bordeaux. The word claret is synonomous with red Bordeaux wine. It is an English word, and not French. Therefore, the final "t" is not silent, and the word is properly pronounced clár-et, not clar-áy. In 1865, 62 of the Bordeaux wines from some 2,000 vineyards were classified as Great Growths (Grands Crus). The classification of 1855 rated the quality of the wine as first, second, third, fourth, or fifth growth (Premier, Seconds, Troisième, Quatrième, or Cinquième Crus). The word "growth" (cru) has nothing to do with the literal meaning of the word. It is unrelated to the time of planting or time of harvest as it is sometimes misconstrued. It is simply a designation of comparative quality among the wines of the classified chateaux. Most of the classified growths do not indicate the growth number on the label. With few exceptions, the label will merely indicate "Grand Cru Classé." Whether the Chateau is classified first or fifth growth is seldom indicated on the label. The classification can be determined only by reference to a printed list which is available in every good wine store and every standard text on wine. A wine classified as fifth growth is obviously not fifth rate since it is superior to the wines of about 1,940 other vineyards. In fact, some good vintages of second or third growths may be as good or better than the same vintage of some of the first growths. Unfortunately, the prices for these great wines are skyrocketing out of sight. A bottle of first growth wine will cost at least $15.00, even for a very mediocre vintage and $25.00 or more for a good vintage. The discriminating buyer may still find some third, fourth, or fifth growths at about $6.00–$8.00 a bottle. Some of the classified growths of the Medoc which are often available at reasonable prices are:

Chateau Kirwan (third growth)
Chateau Pedesclaux (fifth growth)
Chateaux Croizet-Bages (fifth growth)
Chateaux Pontet-Canet (fifth growth)

Thus, for experimentation at reasonable prices, one must look to the wines other than those of the Grand Cru Classé. This means the lower classification of Cru Bourgeois wines of the Medoc or those wines from the Graves, St. Emilion, or Pomerol areas of Bordeaux or shippers' regional wines. Some of these worthy of consideration are:

Chateau Carbonnieux
*Tytell Chevalier
Chateau Phelan-Segur
Chateau Cadet-Piola
Chateau Siran
*Chateau Timberlay
*B & G Pontet-Latour
Vieux-Chateau-Certan

Bordeaux also produces many fine white wines, the best of which come from the areas of Graves and Sauternes. The Graves wines are dry, and the Sauternes are sweet dessert wines. Again, the Chateau bottled wines will generally exceed $5.00 per bottle. The following dry white Bordeaux are representative examples:

A deLuze & Fils, Bordeaux Blanc
Chateau Carbonnieux
*Tytell Chevalier
Chateau Olivier
*Chateau Timberlay
*B & G Pontet-Latour

In the past decade, sweet wines have declined in popular appeal. Therefore, Sauternes wines (including the Barsac Appellation) offer some very good values. Except for the extremely expensive and famous Chateau d'Yquem, many good Sauternes and Barsacs are available at modest prices.

Chateau La Tour Blanche
*Chateau Bel Air
Chateau Broustet

The wines of Burgundy vie with those of Bordeaux for the title of greatest. In recent years, the Burgundy red wines have been losing favor because of their inconsistency and inflated prices. Although a red Bordeaux may occasionally be disappointing, one seldom gets a really poor bottle of Grand Cru or even Cru Bourgeois of red Bordeaux. Even most of the shippers' regional red Bordeaux wines are consistently good. On the other hand, an expensive bottle of red Burgundy may sometimes be little better than a good jug wine. However, the white wines of Burgundy are considered, generally, to be superior to the white wines of Bordeaux.

The famous wines of Burgundy come from the Côte d'Or, the northern part of which is the Côte de Nuits, which produces such great name reds as Romanée-Conti, Chambertin, and Nuits-St.-Georges. The southern portion of the Côte d'Or is the Côte de Beaune which produces the great whites of Mersault and Montrachet and the red Pommard. The remaining areas of Burgundy are Côte Chalonnaise, Maconnais, Beaujolais, and Chablis, which, except for Chablis, produce lesser wines than those of the Côte d'Or.

All of the famous, fine Burgundy wines from the Côte d'Or and Chablis, both red and white, will carry a price tag well over $10.00. If you are flushed some day and wish to try a good Burgundy, look for the Côte de Nuits wines mentioned above or the lesser reds from Gevrey-Chambertin, Clos de Vougeot or Vosne Romanée, or the whites of Mersault, Montrachet or Chablis by a good shipper such as Alexis Lichine, Louis Jadot, Reine Pedauque, Jablouet-Verchere, Louis Latour, or Joseph Drouhin. Even the Chalonnaise, Maconnais, and Beaujolais which can be very nice but never great wines, are difficult to find for under $5.00 a bottle. The following may be found at affordable prices:

Reds:

Marquisat Beaujolais
*Tytell Beaujolais

Faiveley, Mercurey (Chalonnaise)
Jaboulet-Vercherre, Savigny (Côte de Beaune)

Whites:
Domaine de la Maladiere, Chablis
Jablouet-Vercherre, Pouilly Fuisse
*B & G Prince d'Argent

The Rhone Valley still offers many good wines at reasonable prices. The best known Rhones are red except for France's premier rosé wine, Tavel, and a very small production of the white of Condrieu. The most popular of the Rhones is Chateauneuf-du-Pape. The other major wines are Côte Rotie (red) and Hermitage (red and white) which are in the $5.00 to $10.00 bracket. The best buys are the Côtes du Rhone.

Reds:
Domaine de Mont-Redon, Chateauneuf-du-Pape
*B & G Prince Rouge (Côtes du Rhone)
*Jaboulet-Vercherre, Côtes du Rhone

Rosé:
Chateau d'Aqueria, Tavel

Until the past few years, Alsace and the Loire Valley offered many excellent buys in white wines. However, the ridiculous prices of the wines of Bordeaux and Burgundy have increased the demand, and of course, the prices for the Alsace and Loire wines, most of which are now over $5.00 per bottle. If you can find a Loire wine such as a Muscadet, Pouilly Fume, Sancerre, or Vouvray, or an Alsatian Riesling or Gewurztraminer for about $6.00, they are worth trying.

The most famous sparkling wines in the world are those from Champagne. Although all other wine producing countries make sparkling wines, the French insist that champagne comes only from the delimited Champagne area of France. Even other French sparkling wines are not permitted to use the Appellation "champagne," but rather use the designation "mousseux." No member of the European common market may print the word champagne on its sparkling wine label. American sparkling wines have no such restriction and, therefore, are often referred to as champagne. There are three basic processes for making sparkling wine; Champenoise, Charmat, and carbonization. In the Champenoise process the wine is fermented in the bottle in which it is ultimately sold resulting in a wine with small, long-lasting bubbles. It is also the most expensive of the three processes. In the Charmat process the wine is fermented in bulk in large sealed tanks, then transferred to the bottle. Although it is generally considered to be inferior to the Méthode Champenoise, the Charmat process has proved to be very satisfactory and produces some creditable wines at prices substantially lower than those made by the Méthode Champenoise.

All French champagne is made by the Méthode Champenoise and is expensive. It is unlikely that a bottle of French champagne can be purchased for less than $10.00 and more likely, that it will cost at least $15.00 to $25.00. Champagne is made in different styles – from very dry to sweet and is designated brut (the driest), extra-sec (extra dry), sec (dry), demi-sec (semi-sweet), and doux (sweet). There are many excellent champagne producers whose wines are available throughout most of the United States, among whom are Bollinger, Mumm, Möet & Chandon, Piper-Heidsieck, Taittinger, and Charles Heidsieck. Although most champagne is almost colorless, the predominant grape variety in the champagne area is the black-skinned Pinot Noir. In most cases the white Chardonnay or other minor white grape varieties are blended with the Pinot Noir. In some cases, only white grapes are used to produce a blanc de blancs (white of whites) wine.

Germany

Germany, compared to the other major wine-producing countries, produces relatively small quantities of wine. The total wine production of Germany is only about one-tenth that of France or Italy. Approximately 85% of the German wines are white, and are undoubtedly among the great white wines made. They are typified by a strong flowery bouquet, which may seem almost to fill the room when a bottle is first opened. They are produced with a dedication unequalled in any other wine country. Many of the best vineyards are planted on rugged, steep mountainsides where no other agricultural products would survive. Because of the steep inclines, it is impossible to use mechanized equipment and most of the vineyard work is performed manually. With the Germans, wine production is as much an art as it is a commercial enterprise. They are perfectionists, and therefore, their great wines are very expensive. But there are many German white wines of good everyday quality which are still modestly priced. German red wines are considered of little merit in the wine world and are seldom exported.

The German Wine Law of 1971 established three basic quality classifications. They are, in ascending order of quality: tafelwein (table wine); qualitätswein (quality wine); and qualtitäswein mit prädikat (quality wine with attributes). Tafelwein is the lowest classification for ordinary wines. Qualitatswein comes from a particular area, the grape variety is controlled, and it must bear a control number. The law permits the addition of sugar (chaptalisation) to raise the alcoholic content of tafelwein and qualitätswein. Qualitätswein mit prädikat is the highest classification. It has the same controls as qualitätswein plus the added restriction that sugar may not be added to bring the wine up to the required minimum alcoholic content of nine and a half percent. The following words on the label indicate the degree of sweetness of the wine. Kabinett designates the driest of the wines. Spatlese means "late picking" and indicates wine made from grapes which are allowed to ripen fully on the vine, and therefore, produces a sweet wine. Auslese means "select picking" and designates a wine made from individually selected bunches of fully-ripened grapes and produces a sweeter and higher quality wine than spatlese. Beerenauslese means "berry select picking" and denotes a wine made from individually selected grapes from overripe bunches and produces a very sweet and complex wine. Trockenbeerenauslese means "dry berry, selected picking" and indicates a wine made from individually selected grapes which are overripe and almost as dry as raisins, resulting in the sweetest, most complex and most expensive of all German wines.

The Trockenbeerenauslese wine is always produced from grapes which have been attacked by a fungus called Edelfaule (the noble rot, known as Botrytis Cinera in France). This fungus penetrates the grape without breaking the skin and increases its sugar content by reducing the water content. The wine from such grapes is high in alcohol and almost syrupy, much like a liqueur.

There are two major wine areas in Germany. One is the Mosel (Moselle) which includes the Saar and the Ruwer. The labels of Mosel bottles will read "Mosel-Saar-Ruwer." The other is the Rhine which includes the district of the Rheingau, the Rheinhessen, the Nahe, and the Rheinfalz (also called the Palatinate). All of the great wines of Germany are produced from the Riesling grape in the Mosel-Saar-Ruwer and in the Rheingau. The Rheinhessen, Nahe, and Rheinfalz are planted with the Sylvaner grape producing wines of good but lesser quality than the Riesling. None of the wines from the Mosel or the Rhine are really dry, and therefore, they are usually more appropriate after dinner or between meals than as a complement to food. However, the lesser wines such as Liebfraumilch, Moselblumchen or Zeller Schwarze Katz, or the Kabinett or Spatlese categories are quite satisfactory with many seafood dishes. Many German wines, especially in the higher categories of Auslese, Beerenauslese, and Trockenbeerenauslese, because of their high sugar content, are exceptions to the rule that white wines should be drunk young. These classifications will improve with a few years of aging and some of the exceptional vintages have been known to live for many decades.

Mosel:

Anheuser, Bernkastaler
Deinhard, Green Label
*Kreusch, Moselblumchen
*Kreusch, Crover Nacktarsch
Piesporter-Michelsberg
Graff, Wehlener Sonnenuhr

Rhine:

*Little Rhine Bear, Liebfraumilch

Deinhard, Johannisberger
Carl Sittman, Bechtheimer Pilgerpfad
Josef Stinbach, Bornheimer Trappenberg
Sichel, Rudesheimer

All of the above listed wines come in the typical German wine bottle. (Figure 12) The Mosel bottle will be green and the Rhine bottle, brown, but both will have the same basic shape. Although there is not an outstanding vineyard in Germany which grows grapes for the production of sparkling wines, there are a number of producers who make them. German sparkling wines (called sekt) are quite good at one-half to one-third of the price of French champagne. One of the best known and readily available in the United States is Henkell Trocken Sekt which should be purchased for about $8.00 a bottle.

Italy

Italy is one great vineyard from the Alps to the southern-most part of Sicily and produces more wine than any other nation in the world. The ancient Greeks called the Italian peninsula "Enotria," the land of wine. Over 2,000 different wines are produced. Italian wine imports of America are more than double the French or German imports and constitute over sixty percent of all the wines imported. This is not without reason. The ever-increasing prices of French, German, and even many of the good California varietal wines have caused the consumer to look elsewhere for good wine at reasonable prices. Italy has been able to meet that demand. It offers a wide variety of red, white, and rosé wines, sparkling wines, and fortified wines at affordable prices. The best Italian wine will rival the best French wine at less than one-third the price. Many good Italian reds and whites can be purchased for $2.50 to $4.50 a bottle. Even many of the fine Italian wines will retail for only $5.00 to $8.00 per bottle.

In the past, Italian wines have been the most maligned and underrated wines of the world. Until recently, most American and English wine writers have damned Italian wines with faint

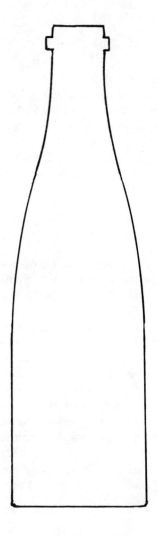

Figure 12

praise. The demeaning of Italian wines prior to the Italian Wine Law of 1963 was not without some justification. Twenty years ago many Italian wine labels were unreliable. The name or origin of the wine printed on the label was too often unrelated to the unpalatable liquid in the bottle. In July 1963, Italy enacted its wine law of Denominazione di Origine Controllata, commonly referred to as DOC. The law is similar to the French law of Appellation Controlée in regulating production per acre, place of origin, grapes grown, and alcoholic content. The consumer is now assured that the bottle contains the wine identified on the label. The purchaser can confidentially buy a bottle of DOC Chianti knowing that it is from the Chianti area of Tuscany and not from some unknown lineage.

Every wine text written over ten years ago would comment about the frivolity and lack of seriousness of Italian wines and winemakers. This is no longer true and never did pertain to the best producers whose standards have been the highest for many decades. Today's wineries are very serious about their products, and many use the most modern and advanced winemaking technology known. Sommelier organizations, whose purpose is to improve the service of wine and promote wine appreciation, exist in most of the cities in Italy. Italian winemakers and consumers are becoming more discriminating and sophisticated with each passing year.

The three major wine areas of Italy are Piedmont, Tuscany, and Veneto. But good and even some great wines are produced in the other seventeen regions. Piedmont is famous for its rich, full-bodied red wines, among which are Barolo, Barbaresco, Gattinara, and Carema and, of course, the renowned, white sparkling wine, Asti Spumante. Barolo has a reputation as the king of Italian wines. It is a long-lived wine and requires a minimum of eight to ten years (usually more) of aging. Barbaresco is similar to Barolo but somewhat lighter and matures sooner. Gattinara is a worthy challenger to Barolo and peaks at about eight to ten years. It is considered by many, including the writer, as one of the finest wines of Italy. The following wines, except for Carema, are not likely to be available for $4.00 a bottle; but all should sell for $5.00 to $10.00 per bottle.

Pio Cesare, Barolo
Villadorio, Barolo
Antoniolo, Gattinara
Bersano, Barbaresco
*Ferrando, Carema
Martini & Rossi, Asti Spumante
Gancia, Asti Spumante

Tuscany is the home of Chianti which is finally receiving the recognition which it truly deserves as one of the world's great wines. A six- to ten-year-old Chianti Classico Riserva from a good producer has few peers. Exceptional vintages have been known to live for fifty years. As a general rule, the straw-covered bottles (fiaschi) of Chianti, although very pleasant if drunk in Italy, should generally be avoided in the United States. It is a wine to be drunk young. Too many of the fiaschi Chiantis sold in America are three years old or more and have lost their youthful freshness. Italy's most expensive wine, Brunello di Montalcino, produced by Biondi-Santi, and many other creditable reds and whites are made in Tuscany.

Reds:
*Brolio, Chianti Classico
*Frescobaldi, Chianti
Ruffino, Riserva Ducale (Chianti Classico Riserva)
Antinori, Chianti Classico Riserva
Brolio, Chianti Classico Riserva
Fattoria dei Barbi, Brunello di Montalcino
Contucci, Vino Nobile di Montepulciano

Whites:
Strozzi, Vernaccia di San Gimignano

The Veneto region produces the very popular Valpolicella and Bardolino red wines and the Soave white wine, which are probably the best known Italian wines, internationally, other than Chianti. These are wines which are light and fruity and meant to be drunk young. The Bardolino and Soave are at their best from one to two years of age, and the Valpolicella, which is a more full-bodied wine, at two to four years of age. Although the Valpolicella and Bardolino are red wines, they may be drunk slightly chilled (not cold). This is especially true of the Bardolino which is much like a heavy rosé wine. The Veneto is also the home of Amarone, one of the truly great wines of Italy. Amarone is a rich, full-bodied, complex, dry red wine which will reach its peak about eight to ten years after the vintage. The Veneto also produces some of the very good sparkling wines of Italy which are just beginning to be exported to America. A Prosecco Spumante (sparkling) of Conegliano or Valdobiaddiene is worth looking for.

Reds:
Bertani, Amarone
*Folonari, Valpolicella
Bertani, Valpolicella-Valpantena
Bolla, Bardolino

Whites:
*Folonari, Soave
Bertani, Soave
Bolla, Soave

More and more wines from the lesser known regions of Lombardy, Sicily, Marche, Apulia, Campania, Lazio, and Emilia-Romagna are finding their way to the United States. Presently the slightly sparkling, red Lambrusco from Emilia-Romagna is extremely popular in America. Although it is produced in both dry and semi-sweet styles, most of the Lambrusco sold here is a semi-sweet variety and not the best example of the wine. Lambrusco is not considered one of Italy's better wines; even the Italians refer to it as the Coca Cola of Italy. It has undoubtedly caught on because of its low price and bubbles. Many of the following wines are excellent buys at modest prices and most of them are now available in the major American markets.

Reds:
*Negri, Inferno or Grumello or Sassella (Lombardy)
Duca di Salaparuta, Corvo (Sicily)
Mastroberardino, Taurasi (Campania)
*Umani Ronchi, Rosso Conero (Marche)
Cirillo-Farrusi, Torre Quarto (Apulia)
Rallo, Segesta (Sicily)

Whites:

*Melini, Orvieto (Umbria)
*Fazi-Battaglia, Verdicchio (Marche)
Mastroberardino, Lacryma Christi (Campania)
*Fontana Candida, Frascati (Lazio)
Duca di Salaparuta, Corvo (Sicily)

Rosés:

Rivera, Castel del Monte (Apulia)
Leone de Castris, Five Roses (Apulia)

United States

It has been said that the American wine industry is still in its infancy. Perhaps adolescence would be a better description, because it is rapidly approaching mature adulthood. The quantity of wine produced has grown dramatically in the past decade. Wineries are being established and new vineyards planted throughout all sections of the country. The quality of American wines has improved to the point where many compare favorably with the great wines of Europe. Many states have relaxed their wine laws to encourage the expansion of their wine industries. Of course, the federal government is also in the act through the Bureau of Alcohol, Tobacco and Firearms (BATF). (Only in America would the incongruity exist of the same agency which regulates firearms and tobacco also regulates wine. Apparently, we have not yet completely repudiated the ignoble experiment of Prohibition nor our puritanical attitude toward alcohol in any form.) The BATF a few years ago proposed labelling regulations, typical of bureaucratic intervention, which were impractical and unrealistic. One proposal would have required a warning on the label somewhat similar to the cigarette warning that wine, beer, and all alcoholic beverages are dangerous to health. Fortunately, rational minds prevailed and no such regulation was promulgated. The final regulation of BATF issued in 1978 controlled blending, varietal names, vintage dates, appellations of origin, and labelling terms such as "estate bottled." Commencing in 1983 a wine may bear the varietal name of the grape only if seventy-five percent or more of the grapes used are the named variety. The prior law required only 51%. The new law also makes provision for procedures to establish delimited geographic appellations of origin similar to the French AOC and the Italian DOC laws. After 1982, the term "estate bottled" will be permitted only if the bottling winery made the wine from grapes grown in vineyards which it either owns or controls within the same viticultural area as the winery. The new law and regulations have remedied many labelling abuses and are generally looked upon with favor by the industry.

California. California is unquestionably America's premier wine state. Its production is about six times more than that of all the other states combined. Understandably, Californians are also the largest wine consumers in the United States. California boasts one of, if not the most, prestigious schools of enology in the world, the University of California at Davis, where enology professors lecture and instruct winemakers throughout the wine-producing countries.

California wineries produce three general categories of wine: generic, proprietary, and varietal. The generics are those which have borrowed the names of their European counterparts, such as Chablis, Sauterne, Chianti, Burgundy, etc. However, they seldom bear any reasonable relationship to their European cousins. If you buy a California Chablis or sauterne, you are assured only that it will be a white wine. It may be dry, sweet, or semi-sweet. One California sauterne will very likely taste completely different from another. Likewise, a California Chianti or Burgundy will bear no resemblance whatsoever to an Italian Chianti or French Burgundy. Again you are assured only that the wine is red and will taste quite different from one producer to another. Nevertheless, there are many pleasant, well-made generic wines which are very good values; among them are:

Reds:
*Beaulieu Vineyards, Burgundy
*Christian Brothers, Burgundy

Whites:

*Paul Masson, Chablis
*Colony, Chablis

A proprietary wine is a winery's trademarked wine, one which is a secret blend of grapes producing a consistent taste from year to year. Proprietary wines are never great but are usually creditable and very drinkable, inexpensive, everyday wines. Some experts look upon proprietary labeling as a step in the right direction away from misleading generic labeling. A California Chablis is not and should not pretend to be a French Chablis. It is an American white wine which can more than hold its own against other inexpensive wines of the world. Most inexpensive California wines are well-made and are superior to most of the ordinary, everyday wines of Europe. Typical of the proprietary wines are:

Reds:

*Paul Masson, Rubion
*Carlo Rossi, Paisano

Whites:

*Paul Masson, Emerald Dry
*Gallo, Rhine Garten

The varietals are those which are named after the grape from which the wine is made: e.g. Cabernet Sauvignon, Barbera, Pinot Blanc, Chardonnay, etc. All of these grape varieties are of the species Vitis Vinifera, which is the noble grape species from which all the great European wines are made. Many of these grapes are thriving and performing extremely well in the California climate. The Cabernet Sauvignon for red wines and the Chardonnay for white wines have been the most successful and are producing superb wines, which, in blind tastings, have often been judged superior to their respective French counterparts from Bordeaux and Burgundy. The Petite Sirah and Barbera grapes are also producing superior wines in the European style, which are only about half the price of the good Cabernets. Likewise, many wineries are making excellent wines from the Johannisberg Riesling, Chenin Blanc, and Pinot Blanc grapes, which are substantially lower in price than the Chardonnays. Zinfandel, perhaps the most ubiquitous of all the Vitis Vinifera, is grown throughout the wine areas of California. It is grown only in America, and no one knows how it got here. Numerous theories have been advanced about its historical habitat, but none have been substantiated; and its origins are still shrouded in mystery. It is a grape which produces very ordinary, jug-type wines in the hot climates of California and extraordinary, long-lived wines in the cool areas. The North Coast counties are making Zinfandels which, after six to ten years of age, will rival the fine Cabernets in their breed and complexity. Perhaps, the most disappointing California varietal has been the Pinot Noir, which has seldom lived up to expectations. Not all varietal wines are great wines, and many of them are over-priced. The quality may vary considerably from one producer to another and even from one vintage to another of the same producer. Some of the consistently good varietals which are nationally distributed are:

Reds:
Beaulieu Vineyards, Cabernet Sauvignon
*Christian Brothers, Cabernet Sauvignon
Sterling, Cabernet Sauvignon
*Sebastiani, Barbera
Louis M. Martini, Barbera
*Charles Krug, Gamay Beaujolais
*Parducci, Petite Sirah
*Cresta Blanca, Petite Sirah
Inglenook, Zinfandel
*Foppiano, Zinfandel
Almaden, Pinot Noir

Whites:
Robert Mondavi, Chardonnay
Beaulieu Vineyard, Beaufort Pinot Chardonnay
*Almaden, Pinot Blanc
*Gallo, French Colombard
*Colony, Chenin Blanc
Charles Krug, Chenin Blanc
Joseph Heitz, Johannisberg Riesling
*Sebastiani, Green Hungarian

Sebastiani, Gewurztraminer
Christian Brothers, Sauvignon Blanc
*Wente Bros., Grey Riesling

Other States. Space does not permit a detailed listing of wines of all the wine producing states of America. Until the past ten or fifteen years, most American wines (other than California) were made from the specie Vitis Labrusca grapes which are indigenous to America (not to be confused with the Lambrusco wine of Italy). These wines were generally considered by most experts to be inferior wines, lacking in the finesse and quality of the European and California wines. The Labrusca grape produces a wine with a taste commonly referred to as "foxy," which can best be described as the taste of Welch's Grape Juice. Typical types of Labrusca grapes used in winemaking are the Concord, Catawba, Niagara, Delaware, and Isabella. In recent years many states have planted and are making wines, with varying degrees of success from Vinifera or French Hybrid grapes, which are a cross of Vinifera and Labrusca or other American species. Generally, their white wines have been more successful than their reds, but both are continually improving and deserve to be watched and tasted. Some of the more successful and best known hybrids are Chelois, Baco Noir, and Seyval Blanc. It may not be too many years until the quality of some of these wines will rival that of many of the California wines.

Every wine buff should be aware of the established wineries of New York and Ohio, and the growing wine industries in Oregon, Washington, Missouri, New Jersey, Maryland, Pennsylvania, and many other states. The best known wineries of New York are Bully Hill Vineyards, Gold Seal Vineyards, Pleasant Valley Wine Company, Taylor Wine Company, Vinifera Wine Cellars and Widmer's Wine Cellars. Boordy Vineyards produces wines in New York, Maryland, and Washington. The best known of the Ohio wineries is Meier's Wine Cellars.

Spain

Spain is another country whose wines are just beginning to

receive the recognition to which they are entitled. Everyone is familiar with Spain's great fortified wine, sherry. There are few people who have not tasted, or at least heard of, the sweet Harvey's Bristol Cream Sherry. But the best sherries are dry and fall into the category called "Fino," which are always light gold colored wines. They are delicate wines to be drunk young and chilled as an aperitif. All other sherries are heavier, darker in color and range from dry to very sweet and should be drunk at room temperature. Amontillado will be sweeter than Fino but will not be as sweet as a cream sherry which is classified as an Oloroso. Many sherries do not use the words Fino, Amontillado, or Oloroso on the label. Many will use such terms as "medium dry," "medium sweet," "cream," "pale," etc. Only by tasting can one determine which style or styles are personally most appealing. All sherries are blended wines and carry no vintage date; and a particular producer's sherry will taste the same year after year.

The popularity of Spain's renowned fortified wine has overshadowed its excellent table wines from the Rioja area. Both white and red wines are produced in the Rioja, but the reds are considered better than the whites. Both are good value for the price. The reds are heavy, rich wines of some complexity and are worth laying down. They are exceptionally long-lived and some have been known to survive for over fifty years. The Riojas, red or white, from any of the following producers will be good wines at very modest prices.

* Marques de Riscal
  Marques de Murrieta
  Frederico Paternino
  Bodegas Bilbainas
* AGE Bodegas Unidas (Siglo)
  Bodegas Rioja Santiago (Yago Condal)

The Panades (also spelled Penedes) area of Spain has one winery, Bodegas Torres, whose excellent wines are generally available in the United States.

* Torres, Sangre de Toro (red)
* Torres, Vina Sol (white)

Portugal

Most Americans are familiar only with the Portuguese rosé wines of Mateus and Lancers, which will be found on almost every restaurant wine list in the United States. Serious wine drinkers consider these wines over-priced and too sweet to drink with most foods. The extensive advertising campaigns of these two wines have detracted from some of the best wine buys available in today's market. The Portuguese Dao (red or white) and Vinho Verde (white) are excellent table wines known only by a few Americans. Wine writer, Hugh Johnson, said, "I have never come across a bad red Dao, either there or abroad." A well-chilled, young Vinho Verde, with its slight sparkle, is a delightful wine with seafood or light dishes. Although its distribution is somewhat limited, Serradayres is another Portuguese red wine worth seeking out. The following wines are exceptional values.

*Grao Vasco, Dao (red or white)
*Casal Garcia, Vinho Verde (white)
*Carvalho, Ribeiro & Ferreira, Serradayres (red)

No discussion of Portuguese wines, even one as brief as this, can omit mention of the fortified wines of port and Madeira. Ruby and tawny ports are blended, undated red wines. Ruby port is the color the name implies and is the youngest and least expensive of the port wines. Tawny port has spent as many as fifteen years in wood and fades in color but achieves a smoothness unattainable in a ruby port. In especially good years when the grapes have had the benefit of perfect weather, the shippers will declare a vintage. A vintage port is an unblended wine produced only from grapes of a single vintage year. It has been called the aristocrat of port wines and should be laid down for fifteen to twenty years before drinking.

Madeira is perhaps the longest lived wine made and may not fade even after one hundred years. Madeira wines are categorized in ascending order of sweetness from Sercial (dry), Verdelho (semi-sweet), Bual (or Boal) (sweet) to Malmsey (very sweet). Madeira has often been aptly described as having a smoky, burnt taste.

Port and Madeira are after dinner wines except for the Sercial or Verdelho Madeira which may be served before a meal. The Bual or especially the Malmsey Madeira are excellent complements to a cup of coffee after dinner.

Other Countries

Many good wines are produced in Austria, Hungary, Yugoslavia, Greece, Romania, Switzerland, Bulgaria, North Africa, South Africa, Australia, and South America. Because of the inflated prices of so many of the wines of France, Germany, and California, many of these exotic wines are finding a market in the United States. Undoubtedly, more and more of them will be imported unless the traditional wines return to more realistic prices. Some are similar to traditional wines but others may taste strange or unlike any classic French, German, or California wine. However, if they are drunk for their intrinsic merit, without trying to compare them with familiar wine styles and tastes, they open a new world of wine tasting experiences. Most of them can be purchased for under $5.00, many for $3.00 to $4.00 a bottle.

Reds:
Achaia Clauss Demestica (Greece)
Adriatica Cabernet (Yugoslavia)
Reserve du Domaine Cabernet (Argentina)
Concha y Toro, Cabernet (Chile)
Egri Bikaver (Hungary)
Paradale, Hermitage (Australia)
B. Seppelt & Sons, Shiraz-Cabernet (Australia)

Whites:
Kutschera & Sohne, Steiner Katz (Austria)
Concha y Toro, Riesling (Chile)
Adriatica Rizling (Yugoslavia)
Achaia Clauss, Santa Helena (Greece)

Magazines and Wine Guides

American Wine Society Journal. AWS Inc., 4218 Rosewold Avenue, Royal Oak, MI 48073.

House publication of the Society devoted primarily to American wines with an emphasis on Eastern wines and wine making.

The Consumer Wine Letter. 21 Oak Street, Irvington, NY 10533.

An 8½″ by 11″ "newsletter" publication with current wine news, topical articles, and suggested good buys of wines of the world.

Decanter Magazine. P.O. Box 4423, Burbank, CA 91502.

Very, very British. Some writers have somewhat snobbish preference for French wines, but recent issues have been extolling virtues of Italian, Spanish, and Portuguese wines. Letters to editors take delight in disagreeing, in typical English fashion, with some of the snob writers.

The Friends of Wine. Les Amis Du Vin, 2302 Perkins Place, Silver Spring, MD 20910.

General wine magazine. Somewhat commercial, however, a very creditable publication with authoritative and well-written articles.

Italian Wines and Spirits. P.O. Box 1130, Long Island City, NY 10101.

Although its avowed purpose is to promote Italian wines in the United States and Canada, it is reasonably objective and extremely informative, well-organized and beautifully illustrated. A must for devotees of Italian wines.

Vintage Magazine. P.O. Box 11779, Philadelphia, PA 19101.

Contains no commercial advertising and considers itself the "voice of the wine consumer." A good, broad-based, general wine magazine without any emphasis on any part of the wine world.

Wines and Vines. 703 Market Street, San Francisco, CA 94103.

A trade publication for wine makers and producers.

The Wine Spectator. 305 E. 53rd Street, New York, NY 10022.

A semi-monthly wine newspaper with latest developments in the world of wine and wine-related news.

Wine World. 15101 Keswick Street, Van Nuys, CA 91405.

Another good, broad-based wine magazine covering wines of the world.

Appendix B

Winery Newsletters

Almaden Vineyards, Alcoa Building, 1 Maritime Plaza, San Francisco, CA 94111.
Buena Vista Winery, 18000 Old Winery Road, Sonoma, CA 95476.
Burgess Cellars, Box 282, St. Helena, CA 94574.
Concannon Vineyard, Box 432, Livermore, CA 94550.
Geyser Peak Winery, 2351 Powell Street, San Francisco, CA 94133.
Inglenook Winery, P.O. Box 19, Rutherford, CA 94573.
Hanns Kornell Winery, Box 249, St. Helena, CA 94574.
Charles Krug Winery, St. Helena, CA 94574.
Parducci Winery, 501 Parducci Road, Ukiah, CA 94582.
The Pleasant Valley Wine Co., Hammondsport, NY 14840.
Sebastiani Vineyards, Box AA, Sonoma, CA 95476.
Souverain Winery, Box 528, Geyserville, CA 95441.
St. Michelle Vintners, Box 3584, Seattle, WA 98124.
Warner Vineyards, PawPaw, MI 49079.

Appendix C

Trade Commissions

French Food and Wine Information Center, 1350 Avenue of the Americas, New York, NY 10019.

German Information Bureau, 3rd Floor, 99 Park Avenue, New York, NY 10016.

Italian Wine Promotion Center, 499 Park Avenue, New York, NY 10022.

New York State, Department of Agriculture and Markets, Building 8, State Campus, Albany, NY 12235.

The Rioja Wine Information Bureau, 770 Lexington Avenue, New York, NY 10021.

Sonoma Valley Wineries, Box 1197, Healdsburg, CA 95448.

Wine Information Bureau, Claremont, Western Australia.

Wine Institute, 165 Post Street, San Francisco, CA 94108.

Appendix D

Basic Wine Library

Johnson, Hugh. *Wine.* New York: Simon and Schuster, 1975.
Johnson, Hugh. *The World Atlas of Wine.* New York: Simon and Schuster, 1978.
Lichine, Alexis. *Encyclopedia of Wines & Spirits.* New York: Alfred A. Knopf, 1968.

Other Recommended General Wine Books

Adams, Leon D. *The Commonsense Book of Wine.* New York: David McKay Company, Inc., 1971.
Durkin, Andrew. *Vendange.* New York: Drake Publishers, Inc., 1972.
Fadiman, Clifton and Aaron, Sam. *The Joys of Wine.* New York: Harry N. Abrams, Inc., 1975.
Griffin, Galen. *The Pocket Guide to Wines.* Brookeville, Maryland: Brooke Meadow Press, 1971.
Grossman, Harold J. *Grossman's Guide to Wines, Spirits, and Beers.* New York: Charles Scribner's Sons, 1964.

Johnson, Hugh. *Pocket Encyclopedia of Wine.* New York: Simon and Schuster, 1978.

Leedom, William S. *The Vintage Wine Book.* New York: Random House, 1963.

Massee, William Edman. *An Insider's Guide to Low-Priced Wines.* New York: Doubleday & Company, Inc., 1974.

Roberts, Jeremy and Northy, Jose. *The Wines of the World.* New York: Bounty Books, 1974.

Sichel, Allan. *The Penguin Book of Wines.* Baltimore, Maryland: Penguin Books, 1972.

Torbert, Harold C. and Frances B. *The Complete Wine Book.* Los Angeles, California: Nash Publishing, 1971.

Waldo, Myra. *The Pleasures of Wine.* New York: Gramercy Publishing Company, 1963.

Yoxall, H. W. *The Enjoyment of Wine.* New York: Drake Publishers Inc., 1972.

Recommended Specialized Wine Books

Adams, Leon D. *The Wines of America.* Boston, Massachusetts: Houghton, Mifflin Company, 1978.

Blumberg, Robert S. and Hannum, Hurst. *The Fine Wines of California.* New York: Doubleday & Company, Inc., 1971.

Chroman, Nathan. *The Treasury of American Wines.* New York: Crown Publishers, Inc., 1975.

Dallas, Philip. *The Great Wines of Italy,* New York: Doubleday & Company, Inc., 1974.

Durac, Jack. *Wines and the Art of Tasting.* New York: E. P. Dutton & Co., Inc., 1974.

Layton, T. A. *Wines of Italy.* London: Harper Trade Journals LTD., 1961.

Lichine, Alexis. *Wines of France.* New York: Alfred A. Knopf, 1969.

Lucia, Salvatore Pablo. *Wine and Your Well-Being.* New York: Popular Library, Inc. 1971.

Massee, William E. *Massee's Guide to Wines of America.* New York: E. P. Dutton & Co., Inc., 1974.

Melville, John. *Guide to California Wines.* San Carlos, California: Nourse Publishing Company, 1968.

Read, Jan. *The Wines of Spain and Portugal.* New York: Hippocrene Books, Inc., 1974.

Roncarati, Bruno. *Viva Vino* (D.O.C. Wines of Italy). London: Wine and Spirit Publications, 1976.

Schoonmaker, Frank. *The Wines of Germany.* New York: Hastings House, 1970.

Simon, Andre L. *The History of Champagne.* London: Octopus Books Limited, 1971.

Simon, Andre L. *The Noble Grapes and the Great Wines of France.* London: Octopus Books Limited, 1972.

Wildman, Frederick S., Jr. *A Wine Tour of France.* New York: Random House, 1976.

WINE TASTING EVALUATION CHART

Date: _____ Place: _____

Type of Wine: _____

Wine	Color Clarity (1)	Aroma Bouquet (4)	Flavor Taste (4)	Body Feel (3)	Balance (3)	After-taste (3)	Overall (2)	Totals	
								My Score	Group Score
1.									
2.									
3.									
4.									
5.									
6.									
7.									
8.									

WINE TASTING

PLACE: _____   DATE: _____

Tasting Chart

WINE	VINEYARD OR SHIPPER	COUNTRY	APPROXIMATE PRICE
1. Vinho Verde	Casal Garcia	Portugal	$3.75
Notes:			
2. Soave	Bolla	Italy	4.25
Notes:			
3. Piesporter Goldtropfchen	Franz Weber	Germany	5.00
Notes:			
4. Rioja–1978	Marques de Riscal	Spain	4.00
Notes:			
5. Chianti Classico Riserva–1974	Nozzole	Italy	6.50
Notes:			
6. Bordeaux–Medoc 1972	Chateau Pedesclaux	France	8.50
Notes:			
7. Cabernet Sauvignon 1974	Beaulieu Vineyards	California	6.50
Notes:			

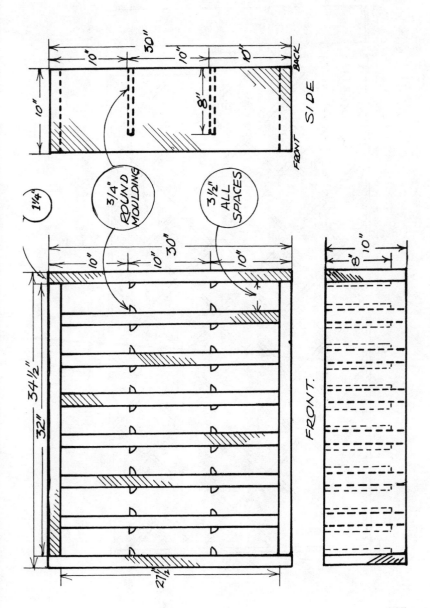

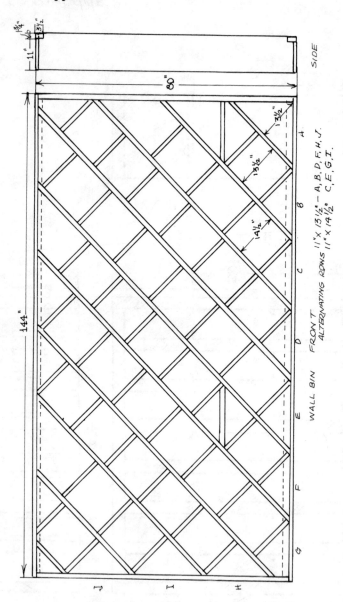

SIDE

13½"

13½"

14½"

80"

144"

¾"

½"

3½"

11"

A B C D E F G

J I H

WALL BIN   FRONT
ALTERNATING ROWS 11" X 13½" — A, B, D, F, H, J.
                  11" X 14½"   C, E, G, I.

Bottle Rack

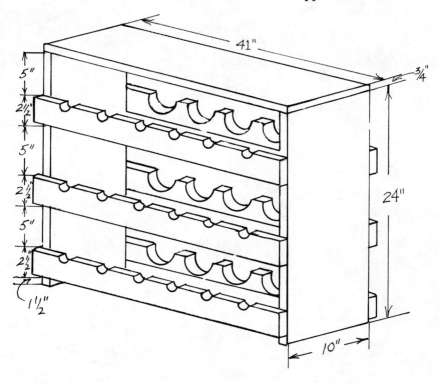

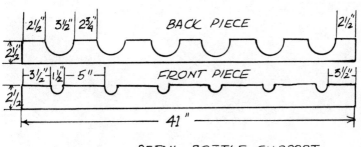

DETAIL BOTTLE SUPPORT
PIECES   SCALE 1/8" = 1"

Detail Bottle Support Pieces

Appendix G

VINEYARD	– Frescobaldi, Nipozzano
VINTAGE	– 1966
PURCHASED	– 11/21/73
AMOUNT PURCHASED	– 5 bottles
PRICE	– $2.77 (less 5%)
WHERE PURCHASED	– Berwyn State Store
IMPORTER	– The Jos. Garneau Co., N.Y.C.

12/1/73   Drank with spaghetti. Wine was excellent for the price; smooth, full-bodied but light, good aftertaste and beautiful ruby color. Improved more as bottle remained open. Very, very good after being opened two or three hours. Certainly worth buying more. Typical good Chianti taste. Probably as good as any Chianti Classico I have tried.

12/8/73   See notes under 1970 Bolla of this date.

1/26/74   Compared with Ruffino Riserva Ducale (1966) and Nozzole Riserva (1967). Better than the Nozzole but not as good as the Ruffino. However, at the price this is an *excellent* buy. Full-bodied, smooth, good aftertaste. Probably better than the Soderi Chianti Classico. This wine only slightly inferior to the Ruffino; lacking the richness and character of the Ruffino. However the Ruffino is almost twice the price.

France – Bordeaux Red
Margaux

VINEYARD	– Chateau Kirwan
VINTAGE	– 1966
PURCHASED	– August, 1971
AMOUNT PURCHASED	– 3 bottles
PRICE	– $4.71 per bottle
WHERE PURCHASED	– Paoli State Store
IMPORTER	– Dreyfus, Ashby & Co., N.Y.C.

9/21/72   Drank bottle with filet mignon. Wine excellent. Smooth, full-bodied, strong aftertaste. Books say that Margaux wines are delicate with much finesse. I did not find this wine "delicate." I thought it quite full-bodied and *almost* heavy. I thoroughly enjoyed it. I consider it an excellent example of an excellent Bordeaux wine.

11/14/72   Drank bottle with prime ribs of beef to celebrate John's getting his real estate salesman's license. My comments above are confirmed. Wine was very good. Full-bodied and good aftertaste. Suspect that more bottle age would improve wine even more.

France—Burgundy—Red
Mercurey

SHIPPER	—Joseph Faiveley
VINTAGE	—1969
PURCHASED	—5/29/74
AMOUNT PURCHASED	—6 bottles
PRICE	—$6.00
WHERE PURCHASED	—S. S. France

7/20/74 Wine disappointing; lacked body, nose and smoothness of good Burgundy. Slightly sharp and ordinary; almost like a Beaujolais.

11/10/74 Better than Dreyfus-Ashby St. Emilion 1969 with which I compared it. However lacking in body and fullness of good Burgundy. More like a heavy Beaujolais than a good Burgundy. Somewhat watery. Not worth price but pleasant. Much better than first notes indicate.

11/13/75 Drank with broiled lamb chops and noodles Romanoff. Wine excellent. I'm amazed at prior notes. Wine was smooth, rich, good nose, good aftertaste, velvety, but slightly sweet. Sufficient tannin to last a few more years. Obviously wine needed rest from rocking and rolling of ship. Typical good Burgundy flavor. A very, very good wine.

California—Red
Cabernet Sauvignon

VINEYARD	– Beaulieu Vineyards
VINTAGE	– 1969
PURCHASED	– 2/3/72
AMOUNT PURCHASED	– 10 bottles
PRICE	– $3.22/bottle (less 5% discount)
WHERE PURCHASED	– Berwyn State Store

1/3/74   Drank with beef burgundy. Very good. Typical cabernet taste without typical California wine flavor or aroma. Crisp, clean taste of good French Bordeaux wines but much heavier than good Bordeaux. Will probably improve even more with a few more years of age.

3/12/74   Drank with roast beef and compared with Louis Martini 1968 Cabernet. B.V. was much better. The Martini tasted like a California wine, the B.V. like a French Bordeaux. Although this B.V. not comparable to the B.V. Private Reserve, it is very good and might improve substantially with age. Dark in color, full-bodied, dry, good aftertaste, and "cigar box" flavor. *Must buy more.* The best of the California wines I have yet tasted except for the B.V. Private Reserve.

6/1/74   Drank with charcoaled steak. Wine excellent. Dark color, but clear. Dry yet extremely smooth and excellent aftertaste. Real cabernet flavor. Better than most French regional or shipper Bordeaux. Probably close to its peak but may still continue to improve.

9/22/74   Had audacity to compare wine with Ch. Mouton-Rothschild (1968). Tom & Joann Campbell were here for dinner. Had charcoal steak. The B.V. was better than the Mouton much to my surprise. The Mouton was disappointing even for a 1968. (See notes under Mouton-R for same date.) The B.V. was very good; full-bodied with interesting character. I believe it is still improving.

1/5/75   Drank with charcoaled steak and compared with L.M. Martini cabernet 1968. (See notes of same date under Martini.) The B.V. had much more body, aftertaste and stronger bouquet and aroma. B.V. was richer. But both very good wines.

2/16/75   Drank with prime rib. Wine was disappointing. Not equal to above comments. Wine somewhat watery and dull. In view of above notes, must have been a poor bottle.

Glossary

Acetic: taste of vinegar.

Acidic: taste of acid. Necessary to good wine, but must be in balance with alcohol, tannin, and fruit.

Aftertaste: the lingering smell and taste after swallowing the wine.

Aperitif: an appropriate wine before dinner (instead of the cocktail) e.g. dry sherry, champagne, vermouth or the same wine as the wine being served for dinner.

Appellation Contrôlée: French wine law guaranteeing place of origin of the wine.

Aroma: the odor of the grape; the fruity smell of the wine.

Aromatic: aroma and flavor of herbs. (See Spicy.)

Astringent: mouth puckering quality caused by tannin.

Baked: description of flavor of wine from hot sunny climates.

Balanced: harmonious combination of acid, tannin, fruit, and alcohol.

Big: full-flavored, strong in alcohol, acid, and tannin.

Bitter: self-explanatory. But not to be confused with acid or tannin.

Blended: the mixing of wines from different years; or the mixing of various grape varieties.

153

Body: the density, fullness, or viscosity of a wine.

Bottle: under metric system 750 milliters (¾ liter). Formerly, about 24 ounces to 25.6 ounces.

Bouquet: fragrance of the volatile esters and aldehydes (vapors) emanating from a wine.

Bourgogne: French word for Burgundy.

Breathe: exposing the wine to the air and allowing the oxygen to react upon the wine.

Breed: that quality of distinction recognizable in a well-made wine from a great vineyard and winery.

Brilliant: favorable self-explanatory quality of color and appearance. Similar to quality of brilliance of a diamond.

Browning: the change of color of a red wine to a brownish red and a white wine to brownish yellow. Results from aging of wine. The older the wine, the "browner" it becomes. Usually a desirable attribute of good red wines but undesirable in most white wines.

Brut: driest of champagnes.

Champenoise Method: the natural secondary fermentation in the bottle of sparkling wines which creates the bubbles. (See Charmat process.)

Chaptalisation: process of adding sugar to the must when grapes have inadequate sugar.

Character: good qualities which are distinctive and interesting.

Characteristic: typical of the particular type of wine.

Charmat Process: the making of sparkling wines by allowing the secondary fermentation to take place in very large, sealed glass or stainless steel tanks before bottling. (See Champenoise method.)

Chateau: a French wine estate, or the villa, castle, or country house on the estate.

Chateau Bottled: bottled at the estate where the wine was made.

Claret: red Bordeaux wine. This is an English word, not French. The "t" is pronounced and is not silent.

Classification of 1855: official classification in the year 1855 of the Bordeaux wines of Medoc and Sauternes. Sixty-two of the approximately 2,000 Medoc vineyards were classified as follows:
First Growths – Premiers Crus
Second Growths – Seconds Crus
Third Growths – Troisièmes Crus
Fourth Growths – Quatrièmes Crus
Fifth Growths – Cinquièmes Crus
The labels of most classified wines will not bear words first, second, etc. but will merely say "Grand Cru Classé."

Clean: refreshing without unpleasant odors.

Climat: individual Burgundy vineyard.

Closed: still devoid of character because recent bottling or inadequate time in bottle to develop and mature; tight.

Cloudy: self-explanatory defect in color or appearance of wine.

Cloying: sticky sweet.

Coarse: rough, unbalanced, not smooth.

Color: self-explanatory.

Common: ordinary, but not poor or bad; apt description for many jug wines.

Complex: a wine with numerous nuances of aroma, bouquet, and taste.

Cooperative: an association of wine growers which "pools" the grapes of its members and sells the wine under a common label.

Corkey: disagreeable odor of a bad, deteriorated cork.

Crisp: dry, clean, pleasingly tart.

Cru Classé: (See Classification of 1855.)

Decant: pouring of wine from bottle into carafe or decanter.

Delicate: light wine with charm but not thin.

Demi-sec: very sweet champagne.

Dessert: a sweet after dinner wine to accompany the dessert course.

DOC: Denominazione di Origine Controllata (controlled name of origin), Italian Wine law.

Double Magnum: large bottle holding the equivalent of four bottles of wine.

Dry: opposite of sweet. But, incongruously, sweet when referring to champagne.

Dull: drinkable but uninteresting.

Earthy: taste of the earth in which the grapes were grown.

Elegant: a wine with finesse and style.

Enologist: wine technician, wine scientist.

Enology: study or science of wine.

Enophile: wine lover.

Estate-bottled: bottled at the estate where the wine was made.

Extra dry: dry champagne, but not as dry as brut.

Fiasco: Italian straw covered, flask-shaped bottle. Used for inexpensive Chianti wines and occasionally for Orvieto wines. Plural: fiaschi.

Fine: great, exceptional, superb. Should be used to describe only a truly superior wine not merely a very good wine.

Finesse: exceptional charm, breeding, and delicacy.

Fining: clarification of wine.

Finish: aftertaste.

Flabby: dull, bland, uninteresting, short of acid and/or tannin.

Flat: dull, insipid, short of acid. As to sparkling wine, loss of bubbles, like a flat beer.

Flinty: metallic taste, not necessarily a bad quality. Typical of Chablis.

Flor: literally "flower." The growth of yeast on the top of the casks of sherry wines which imparts the unique flavor to the sherry wines.

Flowery: fragrance of blossoms of flowers. Typical of Mosels.

Fortified: wine to which brandy or alcohol has been added, e.g. vermouth, sherry, port.

Forward: a wine which is maturing sooner than normally anticipated.

Foxy: Taste of eastern U.S. grapes; like grape juice from Concord grape.

Fragrant: attractive scent.

Fresh: still retaining charm of youth.

Frizzante: slight sparkle or effervescence in Italian wines.

Full-bodied: (See Body.)

Generic: a wine using a misappropriated European place name, e.g. California Chablis, Sauterne, Chianti or Burgundy, none of which bear any reasonable relationship to the European wines from such areas.

Generous: a hearty wine, full, rich-bodied.

Grand Cru: literally "great growth"; a wine produced from a high quality vineyard. (See Classification of 1855.)

Grapey: strong aroma and flavor of the fresh unfermented grape.

Grassy: smell of fresh-cut grass; vegetable taste; stalky.

Green: very young, acidic. Term applied either to wine made from unripe grapes or immature wine.

Growth: (See Classification of 1855.)

Hard: high in tannin, will probably improve and mellow with bottle age.

Harsh: sharp (acidic) and highly tannic.

Heavy: strong in alcohol.

Importer: the company which brings the wines from foreign countries into the U.S.A. and distributes them.

Jeroboam: large bottle holding the equivalent of four to six bottles of wine. In Bordeaux, six bottles; in Champagne, four bottles.

Labrusca: American native grape specie.

Lay down: placing bottle on side to keep cork wet and to age.

Legs: the small amounts of wine which adhere to and slide down the side of the glass after swirling. Originally thought to be indicative of the glycerin content of the wine. Currently believed to be indicative of the alcoholic content of the wine.

Light: lacking in body, but not necessarily a bad quality. Typical of Mosel, Bardolino, and Beaujolais.

Little: undistinguished, no character, dull.

Long: desirable lasting aftertaste (a long finish).

Maderized: ozidized; turning brown from old age; Madeira-like taste. A wine that is over-the-hill.

Magnum: large bottle holding the equivalent of two bottles of wine.

Mature: an adequately aged wine, ready for drinking.

Meaty: deep richness and full body; almost chewable.

Mellow: soft and mature.

Mis en bouteilles au chateau: bottled at the estate where the wine was made; estate bottled.

Moldy: self-explanatory; disagreeable taste or aroma.

Mousseux: term used for all French sparkling wines other than champagne.

Must: the word applied to the fermenting grape juice. As to red wines, it includes the fermenting juice, skins, seeds, and stems.

Musty: stale smell from unclean barrel or cork.

Négociant: French wine dealer. Shipper.

Noble: great breed, quality, and distinction. Noble grapes are those of the vitis vinifera species.

Nose: the combination of aroma and bouquet; the smell of the wine.

Old: well past prime or peak.

Oxidized: self-explanatory; maderized.

Peak: a wine which has arrived; one at its apex for drinking; i.e. neither too young nor too old.

Peppery: aromatic smell or taste of green peppers; a biting harshness which may dissipate or become smoother with additional age.

Perfumey: strong fragrance in bouquet.

Petillant: slight sparkle.

Piquant: pleasing tartness of acid in many white wines and some young red wines.

Poor: drinkable but barely; little, if any, merit.

Proprietaire: winery owner (French).

Proprietary: a trademark wine of the producers individual blend. e.g. Paul Masson *Rubion* or *Emerald Dry*; Gallo *Rhine Garten*.

Punt: indentation in bottom of wine bottle.

Purple: the color of many young red wines.

Regional: a wine blended from various growers within a limited area; and not produced from the grapes of a single vineyard or grower.

Rich: combining all the good qualities of body, balance, and flavor.

Robust: full-bodied, heavy but well-balanced.

Rough: coarse; lacking softness or mellowness.

Rounded: well-balanced.

Sec: sweet champagne, but not as sweet as demi-sec. Oddly, is synonomous with dry when referring to champagne.

Sediment: the residue of solids precipitated by most good red wines in the bottle from the aging process.

Sekt: German sparkling wine.

Sharp: stinging bite of acidity.

Shipper: exporter. The reputation of the shipper is especially important in purchasing regional wines.

Short: little or no aftertaste (a short finish).

Silky: soft, smooth texture of wine with high viscosity. Usually referring to sweet white wine.

Smooth: soft, easy to drink; opposite of rough and harsh.

Soft: mellow, well-rounded.

Sommelier: wine steward.

Sour: acetic; vinegar like; undrinkable.

Sparkling: carbonated whether naturally or artificially. (See frizzante, spritzig, petillant, spumante, sekt.)

Spicy: strong herbaceous taste and aroma. Typical of wines made from Gewurztraminer grapes.

Spritzig: slight sparkle or effervescence in German wines.

Spumante: Italian sparkling wine.

Stalky: aroma of grape stems; grassy.

Still wine: non-sparkling wine.

Sulphury: smell of sulphur (SO_2 — rotten eggs).

Sweet: self-explanatory; opposite of dry.

Table wine: still wine to drink with food as opposed to sparkling wine or fortified wines such as port or vermouth.

Tannic: high in tannin, an essential constituent of all good red wines, derived from the skins, pips, and stems of the grapes. An essential element of all long-lived red wines.

Tart: self-explanatory. Excessive acidity.

Thin: watery; lacking body.

Tight: see Closed.

Varietal: wine made primarily from a single grape variety; e.g. Chardonnay, Zinfandel, Barbera, etc.

Velvety: soft, smooth, richer than silky. Typical of a fine Burgundy.

Vin de pays: ordinary, everyday, country wine.

Vinifera: short for vitis vinifera, the species of classical European wine grapes from which the great wines of the world are produced.

Vintage: See chapter 10.

Vintage Chart: See chapter 10.

Woody: taste of barrel; taste of wood.

Yeasty: smell of yeast as in fresh-made bread.